Simply Salads

Featuring Vegetables, Pasta
and Main Dish Salads

Favorite Recipes® Press

Great American Opportunities, Inc./Favorite Recipes® Press

President: Thomas F. McDow III

Editorial Manager: Mary Jane Blount
Editors: Georgia Brazil, Ashlee Brown
Jane Hinshaw, Linda Jones, Mary Wilson
Essayist: Laura Hill
Typography: Pam Newsome, Sara Anglin

This cookbook is a collection of our favorite recipes which are not necessarily original recipes.

Published by: Favorite Recipes® Press, a division of
Great American Opportunities, Inc.
P.O. Box 305142
Nashville, Tennessee 37230

Manufactured in the United States of America
First Printing: 1991, 50,000 copies

Library of Congress Catalog Number: 91-15662
ISBN: 0-87197-301-4

Table of Contents

Nutritional Analysis Guidelines 4

Simply Salads 5

Hello from a Friend 8

Entrée Salads 9

Fruit Salads 25

Pasta Salads 67

Vegetable Salads 79

Salad Dressings 115

Index 123

Nutritional Analysis Guidelines

The editors have attempted to present these family recipes in a form that allows approximate nutritional values to be computed. Persons with dietary or health problems or whose diets require close monitoring should not rely solely on the nutritional information provided. They should consult their physicians or a registered dietitian for specific information.

Abbreviations for Nutritional Analysis

Cal — Calories	Fiber — Dietary Fiber	Sod — Sodium
Prot — Protein	T Fat — Total Fat	gr — gram
Carbo — Carbohydrates	Chol — Cholesterol	mg — milligrams

Nutritional information for these recipes is computed from information derived from many sources, including materials supplied by the United States Department of Agriculture, computer databanks and journals in which the information is assumed to be in the public domain. However, many specialty items, new products and processed foods may not be available from these sources or may vary from the average values used in these analyses. More information on new and/or specific products may be obtained by reading the nutrient labels. Unless otherwise specified, the nutritional analysis of these recipes is based on all measurements being level.

- **Artificial sweeteners** vary in use and strength so should be used "to taste," using the recipe ingredients as a guideline.
- **Artificial sweeteners** using aspertame (NutraSweet and Equal) should not be used as a sweetener in recipes involving prolonged heating which reduces the sweet taste. For further information on the use of these sweeteners, refer to package information.
- **Alcoholic ingredients** have been analyzed for the basic ingredients, although cooking causes the evaporation of alcohol thus decreasing caloric content.
- **Buttermilk, sour cream** and **yogurt** are the types available commercially.
- **Cake mixes** which are prepared using package directions include 3 eggs and ½ cup oil.
- **Chicken**, cooked for boning and chopping, has been roasted; this method yields the lowest caloric values.
- **Cottage cheese** is cream-style with 4.2% creaming mixture. Dry-curd cottage cheese has no creaming mixture.
- **Eggs** are all large.
- **Flour** is unsifted all-purpose flour.
- **Garnishes**, serving suggestions and other optional additions and variations are not included in the analysis.
- **Margarine** and **butter** are regular, not whipped or presoftened.
- **Milk** is whole milk, 3.5% butterfat. Lowfat milk is 1% butterfat. Evaporated milk is whole milk with 60% of the water removed.
- **Oil** is any vegetable cooking oil. Shortening is hydrogenated vegetable shortening.
- **Salt** and other ingredients to taste as noted in the ingredients have not been included in the nutritional analysis.
- If a choice of ingredients has been given, the analysis reflects the first option.

Simply Salads

Until about the middle of the twentieth century, salads were one of those afterthoughts in American cuisine. While we certainly enjoyed salads, most Americans would have described them as, perhaps, a dish of lettuce and tomatoes, a fruit or gelatin concoction or a mixture of cooked vegetables like potatoes. On the whole, they remained an uninspiring—and uninspired—menu item until recently.

With our growing awareness of good health and nutrition, and the increasing availability of excellent fresh produce year-round, however, salads have become a favorite part of the way we eat. What other dish can turn up at breakfast, lunch and dinner, stand in for an appetizer or dessert, garner cheers as a fancy entrée, or be recycled into a delicious snack? Salads are just as at home in a lunchbox or on a picnic as at a formal dinner.

Salads also make healthy eating delicious and simple. Picky eaters seem to be able to manage their veggies better if they're the stars of a crisp salad, or cooked and then tossed in a piquant dressing. And even the heartiest salad can easily be low-fat, low-calorie, low-cholesterol and high in vitamins, minerals, and even protein.

At a time when our lifestyles are so busy, and complicated schedules often make mealtimes less than relaxed, salads are a particularly appealing alternative to the standard meat-and-potatoes dinner that requires a long stint in the kitchen. In fact, often that same meat and potatoes can be incorporated into an easy, prepare-ahead feast to be whisked out of the "frig" at a moment's notice or eaten in shifts, depending on your family's needs.

Why "simply" salads? Today's cooks have a wider selection of ingredients than ever before to choose from in planning salads. Supermarkets abound with greens, vinegars, oils, fruit and vegetables that most of us had never heard of years ago. Specialty stores boast of still newer varieties. With so many good things to choose from, successful salads are simple indeed. And with the growing popularity of grocery salad bars (or the takeout counter of your favorite restaurant) all you may need to do for a knock-out dinner is pick up the basics on the way home and toss them with leftovers from the refrigerator. What could be simpler?

If the wide variety of salad choices is a relatively new development, our taste for salad dates back to ancient times. Interestingly, the word "salad" comes from the Latin "sal," which, of course, means salt. The connection comes from the use of salt as the most common dressing of the simple salads favored by the Romans. As time went on, concoctions of green and leafy vegetables, frequently served with meat or fowl, became popular in Europe.

After the Civil War, food historian John Mariani notes, salads became popularized in this country first in restaurants, where such classics as Waldorf Salad (from the Waldorf Astoria Hotel in New York) were born. Gradually green "salats" as they were often called, grew in popularity, as did ethnic additions such as potato salads, brought here by German immigrants, and the widespread use of tomatoes, favored by Italian-Americans. In mid-century the growing importance of California's outstanding fresh produce and its fresh-from-the-garden cuisine placed salads on the American map for good.

We've organized *Simply Salads* into convenient chapters that take into account the wide variety of ways in which we enjoy salads in our menus today, and the wonderful assortment of ingredients available.

Entrée Salads...

Entrée salads spotlight combinations of meats, poultry, seafood, cheeses and vegetables, served warm and cold, as well as more traditional composed salads that make great lighter entrées. While they go by the name salad, you'll find most of these recipes just as suitable in December as they are in May.

Entrée salads are a wonderful way to include meat and poultry in your diet without centering whole meals around them. They're a perfect way to use leftover grilled or broiled meat (cook a little extra steak or fried chicken next time) and can even be used with takeout "fast food" in some cases.

Fruit Salads...

Our chapter on fruit salads demonstrates just how wonderfully versatile salads can be. Included are fresh fruit recipes, do-ahead canned fruit salads and combinations of both. You'll find gelatin salads, sweet salads and tart salads, salads with creamy dressings and salads that are crunchy and frozen, some that are light and some more substantial. And nearly every fruit flavor and color imaginable.

What's particularly delightful about all this bounty is that many of these fruit salads can be just as easily enjoyed at lunch (or even breakfast) as at dinner, and in many cases make great desserts, and a healthy alternative to heavy sweets.

Pasta Salads...

Pasta salads have become classics in such a short time that commercial mixes are now widely available. Though not nearly as tasty as the homemade variety, they do speak to our need for quick-to-fix foods.

Our pasta salads cover a broad range in tastes and ingredients, from the familiar to the adventurous. All are simple to prepare, and most can be used as either entrées or as side dishes.

Vegetable Salads...

Vegetable salads are, for most of us, "far and away" the favorite salad standby. But if you think there's nothing exciting about that "plain green salad," you have not checked your local supermarket produce section lately.

Arugula, radicchio, mache, sorrel and fennel are spicy newcomers to the American palate, and are wonderful used in combination with less distinctively flavored greens. Easier to find, and extremely versatile, are such once-rare greens as watercress, red and green leaf lettuce, curly endive, escarole, chicory and delicately flavored Bibb and Boston lettuce.

Used together, today's "new" greens give the plain green salad a new status, especially when accented with a new dressing, and unusual, unexpected fruits and vegetables.

Salad Dressings...

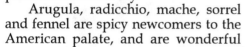

Salad dressings, too, have undergone a virtual revolution lately, and when it comes to such essential ingredients as vinegar and oil, you're only as limited as your imagination.

Vinegar has been a staple in most Western countries since Greek and Roman times, when bowls of vinegar were set out at the table into which diners could dip their bread. The vinegar with which most Americans are familiar is distilled white vinegar, made from grain alcohol diluted with water.

If you have not already done so, try substituting Sherry, rosé, Champagne or other lighter wine vinegars in your dressings. Equally versatile vinegars are herb, fruit, cider and probably most popular of all the newer vinegars, balsamic. Each has its own particular appeal, from the tart but fruity aroma and taste of raspberry to the mellow, woodsy sweetness of balsamic vinegar.

A bit of taste testing will help you choose your own favorites.

Working hard in hand with these new vinegars are a whole pantry full of new oils that have made their appearances in the past few years. Our search for new and improved no-cholesterol dressings has actually led us to rediscover old-fashioned oils some of us had simply forgotten about. Chief among them, of course, is olive oil, that mainstay of European households.

In your looking about, don't neglect to sample some of the newer nut oils, such as walnut, hazelnut or almond oils. These can turn even the most mundane assortment of salad greens into a gourmet treat. Nearly all of these new vinegars and oils can be successfully integrated into your own classic dressings, or used in variations of the recipes we have presented here.

One of the great joys of salad preparation is the creative opportunity afforded when so many ingredients are combined into a single dish. Don't be afraid to vary quantities and combinations to suit your own particular tastes and needs. We've made experimenting even easier by including a bumper crop of salad preparation tips throughout the book, denoted by this apple 🍎 symbol. We think you'll find these ideas, and the recipes that follow, will keep your salad days simple, indeed—and delicious.

"These cookbooks are great! I have a foods class that does a lot of cooking, and the students always select these books over others. They are easy to read, a good format and excellent recipes."

Barbara Grimes, Northeast H. S., Arma, KS

There are some things in life that one just doesn't want to give up—comfortable old easy chairs, favorite snuggly pillows, broken-in walking shoes and Home Economics Teachers Cookbooks from Favorite Recipes® Press. Cookbooks? Yes, cookbooks.

These special cookbooks often become treasured heirlooms handed down from mother to daughter, or maybe we should say from parent to child. Sometimes the pages are dog-eared or marked with floured fingerprints. Many times favorite recipes are critiqued with handwritten notes: "Super for a crowd." or "Even better the next day."

In the past almost 30 years, we've published more than 35 cookbooks, and the sale of these books has earned over $52,000,000 in profits for Home Economics Departments nationwide.

Also in the past 30 years, we know that these cookbooks have become like old, trusted, family friends, and, on at least one occasion, they've been a bone of contention in a property settlement.

It happened in Texas. A couple separated. When they divided up their assets, things went smoothly until the Home Economics Teachers Cookbook collection came up for discussion. Neither wanted to break up the collection, but both wanted the books. Finally the books were divided equally, and "visitation rights" given to each for the books they didn't possess.

All went smoothly for a few months until the gentleman became frustrated with his limited access to the cookbooks. He tried to locate us to order

Thomas F. McDow III
President

more books, but our address had changed. Then, since he had bought the books through home economics fundraising programs, he thought of calling his daughter's former home economics teacher, Lucy Walker (now Vocational Program Director in Amarillo, Texas). Ms. Walker put him in touch with us, and as she remembers, "Those books were his most prized possessions. I was glad I was able to help him with the Favorite Recipes® Press address."

Some of the books were out of print, but we were able to send him many of the books he requested, and he ordered several of our newer titles as well.

Yes, there are just some things in life that one just doesn't want to give up.

We hope this book will become a treasured heirloom in your family and thank you for supporting your local home economics program.

If you have a story about Home Economics Teachers Cookbooks, why not pass it along! Just write to us at: Favorite Recipes® Press, P.O. Box 305142, Nashville, TN 32730.

Salads Salads Salads Salads Salads
Salads Salads Salads Salads Salads
Salads Salads Salads Salads Salads
Salads Salads Salads Salads Salads

ENTREES

SUPER SIMPLE ROAST BEEF SALAD

1½ cups seedless raisins
2 cups roast beef strips
1½ cups pineapple chunks
½ cup chopped celery
½ cup green bell pepper
  strips
¼ cup stuffed green olives
¼ cup slivered almonds
1 tablespoon chopped
  pimento
1½ cups seedless green
  grapes
½ cup sour cream

Soak raisins in warm water to cover for 15 minutes; drain. Place in large salad bowl. Add roast beef, pineapple, celery, green pepper, olives, almonds, pimento, grapes and sour cream; toss to mix. Chill, tightly covered, for 2 hours to overnight. May garnish with coconut and a sprinkle of curry powder. Yield: 6 servings.

*Approx Per Serving: Cal 323; Prot 13 g;
Carbo 48 g; Fiber 5 g; T Fat 12 g;
Chol 36 mg; Sod 268 mg.*

*Lita M. Tabish
Deer Park High School
Deer Park, Washington*

SIRLOIN STEAK SALAD

1½ pounds boneless sirloin
  steak
Garlic powder to taste
Freshly ground pepper to
  taste
Seasoned salt to taste
1 package ranch salad
  dressing mix
1 cup mayonnaise
1 cup sour cream
1 pint cherry tomatoes, cut
  into quarters
4 ounces fresh mushrooms,
  sliced

Season sirloin steak with garlic powder, pepper and seasoned salt. Grill over hot coals or until steak is done to taste. Chill in refrigerator; trim. Slice thinly cross grain. Combine salad dressing mix, mayonnaise and sour cream in bowl; mix well. Chill in refrigerator. Toss steak with enough dressing to coat. Add tomatoes and mushrooms. Add additional dressing if necessary. Yield: 4 servings.

*Approx Per Serving: Cal 781; Prot 36 g;
Carbo 13 g; Fiber 2 g; T Fat 66 g;
Chol 154 mg; Sod 890 mg.
Nutritional information includes
entire amount of dressing.*

*Suzanne Scannell
Aldine Senior High School
Houston, Texas*

CHICKEN SALAD

6 cups chopped cooked
   chicken
1 6-ounce can sliced water
   chestnuts
2 cups slivered almonds
2 cups finely chopped celery
1/2 cup chopped green onions
1 cup seedless green grapes
2 cups mayonnaise
Juice of 2 lemons
1 24-ounce can Chinese
   noodles

Combine chicken, water chestnuts, almonds, celery, green onions and grapes in bowl. Add mixture of mayonnaise and lemon juice; mix well. Stir in noodles. Yield: 15 servings.

Approx Per Serving: Cal 663; Prot 26 g; Carbo 35 g; Fiber 5 g; T Fat 48 g; Chol 72 mg; Sod 686 mg.

Kathryn Jensen
Box Elder High School
Brigham City, Utah

COLD CURRIED CHICKEN SALAD

1¼ cups mayonnaise
1½ teaspoons curry powder
1 teaspoon salt
1/4 teaspoon pepper
1½ tablespoons lemon juice
2 cups cooked rice
2 cups chopped cooked
   chicken
1/4 cup chopped green onions
1/2 cup flaked coconut

Combine mayonnaise, curry powder, salt, pepper and lemon juice in small bowl; mix well. Combine rice, chicken, green onions and coconut in salad bowl; mix well. Add dressing; toss to mix. Yield: 6 servings.

Approx Per Serving: Cal 523; Prot 16 g; Carbo 21 g; Fiber 1 g; T Fat 42 g; Chol 69 mg; Sod 657 mg.

Donna J. Certosimo
Kempsville High School
Virginia Beach, Virginia

 Reduce the calories and fat of mayonnaise by mixing 1/2 cup mayonnaise with 1 cup unflavored yogurt. For fruit salads, mix 1/2 cup mayonnaise with 1 cup flavored yogurt.

CURRIED CHICKEN SALAD

2 cups coarsely chopped
  cooked chicken
1/4 cup sliced water chestnuts
8 ounces seedless green
  grapes, cut into halves
1 8-ounce can pineapple
  chunks, drained
1/2 cup chopped celery
1/2 cup toasted almonds
3/4 cup mayonnaise
1 teaspoon curry powder
2 teaspoons soy sauce
2 teaspoons lemon juice

Combine chicken, water chestnuts, grapes, pineapple, celery and almonds in salad bowl; mix well. Mix mayonnaise, curry powder, soy sauce and lemon juice in bowl. Add dressing to salad; toss to mix. Yield: 4 servings.

Approx Per Serving: Cal 603; Prot 25 g;
Carbo 24 g; Fiber 4 g; T Fat 47 g;
Chol 87 mg; Sod 484 mg.

Patricia Allen
Stafford Senior High School
Falmouth, Virginia

CHICKEN SALAD WITH OLIVES

8 chicken breasts
1 15-ounce can pineapple
  chunks, drained
1 7-ounce jar stuffed green
  olives, drained
5 hard-boiled eggs, chopped
3 stalks celery, finely
  chopped
1 pint mayonnaise-type salad
  dressing

Rinse chicken. Cook chicken in salted water to cover in saucepan until tender. Cool; chop into bite-sized pieces. Combine chicken, pineapple, olives, eggs, celery and salad dressing in bowl; toss to mix. Serve on lettuce-lined salad plates. Yield: 15 servings.

Approx Per Serving: Cal 229; Prot 13 g;
Carbo 12 g; Fiber 1 g; T Fat 15 g;
Chol 105 mg; Sod 600 mg.

Patsy Boyett Ashmore
Pickens County High School
Reform, Alabama

 For a quick salad, mix together cherry tomato halves, crumbled bacon and mayonnaise.

HOT CHICKEN SALAD

2 cups chopped cooked
  chicken
1½ cups chopped celery
¼ cup chopped almonds
1 teaspoon chopped onion
1 teaspoon grated lemon rind
1 tablespoon lemon juice
⅛ teaspoon pepper
⅔ cup mayonnaise
Salt to taste
1 cup shredded Cheddar
  cheese
1 cup crushed potato chips

Combine chicken, celery, almonds, onion, lemon rind, lemon juice and pepper in bowl; mix well. Add mayonnaise; toss to mix. Add salt. Spoon into shallow 1½-quart casserole. Sprinkle with cheese and potato chips. Bake at 375 degrees for 25 minutes or until cheese is bubbly. Yield: 4 servings.

*Approx Per Serving: Cal 600; Prot 30 g;
Carbo 9 g; Fiber 2 g; T Fat 50 g;
Chol 114 mg; Sod 515 mg.*

*Margaret A. Ramsdale
Hutchinson High School
Hutchinson, Kansas*

CHICKEN LIVER SALAD

8 ounces bacon
12 ounces chicken livers
½ cup walnut pieces
6 tablespoons red wine
  vinegar
1 large clove of garlic,
  crushed
1 teaspoon Dijon mustard
¼ teaspoon salt
¼ teaspoon pepper
8 cups bite-sized salad greens
1 medium red onion, thinly
  sliced, separated into rings
½ medium red bell pepper,
  cut into strips

Cut bacon into 1-inch pieces. Cook in skillet until crisp; remove bacon. Sauté chicken livers in bacon drippings for 5 minutes; remove chicken livers. Add walnuts to skillet. Sauté for 1 minute. Drain, reserving ¼ cup drippings. Add vinegar, garlic, mustard, salt and pepper to reserved drippings in skillet; stir until blended. Keep warm over low heat. Combine salad greens, onion and red pepper in salad bowl. Add bacon, chicken livers and walnuts. Add dressing; toss lightly. Serve immediately.
Yield: 4 servings.

*Approx Per Serving: Cal 363; Prot 30 g;
Carbo 11 g; Fiber 3 g; T Fat 23 g;
Chol 551 mg; Sod 477 mg.*

*Jo Ann Medendorp
East Lawrence High School
Hartselle, Alabama*

ORIENTAL FRIED CHICKEN SALAD

4 large fast-food fried
  chicken breasts
1 pound bacon
3/4 cup chopped green onions
1 cup chopped celery
1   8-ounce can sliced water
  chestnuts, drained
1 large head iceberg lettuce,
  chopped
1/3 cup oil
1/3 cup soy sauce
2 tablespoons honey
2 tablespoons catsup
1   3-ounce can chow mein
  noodles

Bone and chop chicken breasts. Cut bacon slices into 1-inch pieces. Fry bacon in skillet until crisp; drain. Combine chicken, bacon, green onions, celery and water chestnuts in bowl; mix well. Chill overnight. Add lettuce to salad; toss to mix. Mix oil, soy sauce, honey and catsup in bowl. Pour over salad. Add chow mein noodles; toss to mix. Yield: 8 servings.

*Approx Per Serving: Cal 460; Prot 26 g;
Carbo 24 g; Fiber 2 g; T Fat 29 g;
Chol 75 mg; Sod 1313 mg.*

*Carol S. Newnam
Guy B. Phillips High School
Chapel Hill, North Carolina*

ORIENTAL SESAME CHICKEN SALAD

4 chicken breasts
1/4 cup sugar
2 teaspoons salt
1 teaspoon MSG
1/4 cup vinegar
1/2 teaspoon pepper
1/2 cup oil
1 head lettuce, chopped
1   1-pound package spinach,
  chopped
3 to 6 green onions, chopped
1   4-ounce package sliced
  almonds
1/2 cup sesame seed, toasted
1   8-ounce can sliced water
  chestnuts, drained
2 or 3   5-ounce cans chow
  mein noodles

Rinse chicken. Cook chicken in water to cover in saucepan until tender. Cool; chop into bite-sized pieces. Combine sugar, salt, MSG, vinegar, pepper and oil in bowl; mix well. Add chicken. Marinate in refrigerator overnight. Combine lettuce, spinach, green onions, almonds, sesame seed and water chestnuts in salad bowl; toss well. Add chicken and marinade; toss lightly. Serve over chow mein noodles. Yield: 6 servings.

*Approx Per Serving: Cal 829; Prot 32 g;
Carbo 64 g; Fiber 10 g; T Fat 53 g;
Chol 41 mg; Sod 2244 mg.*

*Sue Dennis
Huntsville Senior High School
Huntsville, Arkansas*

RAMEN CHICKEN AND CABBAGE SALAD

1/4 cup sugar
1 teaspoon pepper
1 cup oil
2 teaspoons MSG
6 tablespoons rice vinegar
1/2 cup slivered almonds,
    toasted
1/2 cup sesame seed, toasted
2 cooked chicken breasts,
    chopped
1 medium head cabbage,
    chopped
8 green onions, chopped
2 3-ounce packages ramen
    noodles

Combine sugar, pepper, oil, MSG and rice vinegar in bowl; mix well. Combine almonds, sesame seed, chicken, cabbage and green onions in salad bowl; toss to mix. Add dressing; toss well. Add ramen noodles just before serving time; toss to mix. Yield: 6 servings.

Approx Per Serving: Cal 667; Prot 18 g;
Carbo 31 g; Fiber 6 g; T Fat 55 g;
Chol 24 mg; Sod 1833 mg.

Pam Reed
West High School
Torrance, California

THAI MIXED SALAD

1 head iceberg lettuce
2 whole chicken breasts,
    boned, skinned
2 tablespoons oil
1 carrot
1 red bell pepper
1 cup oil
1/3 cup white vinegar
2 tablespoons soy sauce
2 tablespoons smooth peanut
    butter
4 cloves of garlic, minced
1 teaspoon crushed dried red
    chilies

Wash and trim lettuce; drain. Chill in sealed plastic bag until crisp. Cut chicken into thin slices. Sauté in 2 tablespoons hot oil in skillet over high heat for 4 to 5 minutes or until tender. Remove to drain. Cut carrot and red pepper into julienne strips. Stir-fry in pan drippings for 4 to 5 minutes or until tender-crisp. Return chicken to skillet; keep warm. Combine 1 cup oil, vinegar, soy sauce, peanut butter, garlic and red chilies in jar. Cover with lid; shake to mix. Shred lettuce fine to measure 1 1/2 quarts. Layer lettuce, chicken and vegetables on serving plate. Garnish with cilantro and peanuts. Pour half the dressing over salad. Serve with remaining dressing. Yield: 6 servings.

Approx Per Serving: Cal 477; Prot 16 g;
Carbo 6 g; Fiber 2 g; T Fat 45 g;
Chol 33 mg; Sod 410 mg.

Anne VanBeber
L. V. Berkner High School
Richardson, Texas

PERSONAL TACO SALAD

1 pound ground beef
1 medium onion, chopped
1 16-ounce can tomatoes
1 envelope taco seasoning
  mix
1 16-ounce can chili beans
1 16-ounce package tortilla
  chips, crushed
8 ounces Cheddar cheese,
  shredded
1 cup low-fat sour cream
2 cups shredded lettuce
1 large tomato, chopped
1/2 cup sliced green olives
1 cup ranch dressing

Separate ground beef into small pieces in microwave-safe dish; sprinkle with onion. Cover loosely with plastic wrap. Microwave on High for 5 minutes. Stir ground beef to separate. Microwave on High for 1 to 2 minutes longer or until ground beef is no longer pink; drain. Purée canned tomatoes with taco seasoning mix in blender for 5 seconds. Add with chili beans to ground beef. Microwave on High for 5 to 7 minutes or until heated through. Layer tortilla chips, ground beef mixture, cheese, sour cream, lettuce, chopped tomato and olives into 6 salad bowls. Spoon ranch dressing over each salad. May also layer ingredients in 1 large salad bowl and serve. Yield: 6 servings.

Approx Per Serving: Cal 1040; Prot 38 g; Carbo 73 g; Fiber 11 g; T Fat 69 g; Chol 105 mg; Sod 2288 mg.

Becky Beck
Hibriten High School
Lenoir, North Carolina

EASY TACO SALAD

1 pound ground beef
1 envelope taco seasoning
  mix
1 16-ounce can hot chili
  beans
1/2 cup water
1/2 head lettuce, shredded
1 cup shredded Cheddar
  cheese
1 tomato, chopped
1 small onion, chopped
1 16-ounce package tortilla
  chips, crushed

Brown ground beef in skillet, stirring until crumbly; drain. Add taco seasoning mix, chili beans and water. Cook until heated through, stirring occasionally. Layer lettuce, cheese, tomato and onion on individual salad plates. Sprinkle with crushed chips. Top with ground beef mixture. Serve with additional chips. Yield: 4 servings.

Approx Per Serving: Cal 1051; Prot 45 g; Carbo 96 g; Fiber 15 g; T Fat 56 g; Chol 104 mg; Sod 2071 mg.

Nancy M. Love
Fieldale-Collinsville High School
Collinsville, Virginia

TABOULI SALAD

2 cups boiling water
1 cup cracked wheat
1/4 cup canola oil
1/4 cup lemon juice
1 teaspoon salt
1/2 teaspoon pepper
1 cup fresh chopped parsley
1/2 cup chopped green onions
2 tomatoes, chopped
1 teaspoon vinegar
1/2 cup chopped celery
1 medium cucumber,
  chopped
1 cup chopped cooked beef

Pour boiling water over cracked wheat in bowl. Let stand for 1 hour. Drain well in colander. Return to bowl. Add remaining ingredients; mix well. Chill for 2 hours or longer. Serve on lettuce-lined salad plates. Yield: 4 servings.

Approx Per Serving: Cal 370; Prot 15 g; Carbo 41 g; Fiber 11 g; T Fat 17 g; Chol 27 mg; Sod 576 mg.

Nancy Burke
Medical Lake High School
Medical Lake, Washington

RANCH SALAD

1 pound ground beef
1 small head lettuce, chopped
3 or 4 small finely chopped
  green onions
1 cup grated Cheddar cheese
1 15-ounce can ranch-style
  beans
2 tomatoes, chopped
1 6-ounce bottle of Catalina
  salad dressing
1 9-ounce package corn
  chips

Brown ground beef in skillet, stirring until crumbly; drain. Combine lettuce, green onions, cheese and beans in bowl. Add tomatoes and ground beef. Pour salad dressing over salad; toss to mix well. Serve over corn chips. Yield: 4 servings.

Approx Per Serving: Cal 1025; Prot 40 g; Carbo 66 g; Fiber 10 g; T Fat 69 g; Chol 139 mg; Sod 1610 mg.

Evelynn Dyer
DeSoto High School
DeSoto, Texas

 A little dill pickle juice sprinkled on lettuce for taco salad will keep it from tasting dry and "brighten up" the flavor.

MAIN DISH HAM SALAD

1   10-ounce package frozen
     green peas
1/2 teaspoon salt
11/4 cups water
1 cup enriched pre-cooked
     long grain rice
3/4 cup mayonnaise
1 tablespoon grated onion
1/2 cup finely chopped dill
     pickles
3/4 cup thin strips cooked
     ham

Boil peas with salt in water for 5 minutes. Remove from heat. Add rice. Let stand, tightly covered, until cool. Add mayonnaise, onion, pickles and ham; mix well. Chill, covered, until serving time. Serve with lettuce and tomatoes. May use 1/4 pound cooked ham or 1 can cooked ham. Yield: 4 servings.

*Approx Per Serving: Cal 476; Prot 12 g;
Carbo 24 g; Fiber 4 g; T Fat 38 g;
Chol 41 mg; Sod 1342 mg.*

*Lynn Johnson, C.H.E.
Newberry High School
Newberry, South Carolina*

SAUSAGE SKILLET SALAD

11/2 pounds sausage
2 cups cooked minute rice
1   6-ounce can mushrooms
1 medium onion, chopped
6 large hard-boiled eggs,
     chopped
3 tablespoons soy sauce
3 tablespoons Worcestershire
     sauce
2 cups chopped celery
2 cups chopped carrots
1 cup chopped green bell
     pepper
2 cups shredded Cheddar
     cheese

Brown sausage in skillet, stirring until crumbly; drain. Combine sausage, rice, mushrooms, onion, eggs, soy sauce and Worcestershire sauce in large skillet. Simmer for 1 hour, stirring occasionally. Add celery, carrots and green pepper. Cook until just tender-crisp. Stir in cheese. Yield: 10 servings.

*Approx Per Serving: Cal 340; Prot 15 g;
Carbo 16 g; Fiber 2 g; T Fat 24 g;
Chol 174 mg; Sod 851 mg.*

*Shelly Dueser
Derby Middle School
Derby, Kansas*

 When using browned ground beef or sausage added to a salad, rinse the meat under water after draining the drippings. Very few nutrients are lost but a lot of extra drippings are gone.

STUFFED TOMATOES WITH CRAB MEAT DRESSING

6 medium tomatoes
12 ounces cottage cheese
1/3 cup chopped green bell
   pepper
1 tablespoon grated onion
1 tablespoon Worcestershire
   sauce
2 cups mayonnaise
1/2 cup chopped celery
1/3 cup chili sauce
1 6-ounce can crab meat,
   drained

Turn tomatoes upside down. Cut into wedges to but not through bottom. Spread open gently. Combine cottage cheese, green pepper, onion and Worcestershire sauce in bowl; mix well. Spoon into tomato cups. Combine mayonnaise, celery, chili sauce and crab meat in bowl; mix well. Spoon 2 or 3 tablespoonfuls over each tomato. Serve with crackers or breadsticks. May add 1/4 teaspoon cayenne pepper to cottage cheese mixture. Yield: 6 servings.

Approx Per Serving: Cal 657; Prot 15 g; Carbo 14 g; Fiber 2 g; T Fat 61 g; Chol 77 mg; Sod 985 mg.

Willetta Swoope
Armstrong Junior High School
Starkville, Mississippi

SPANISH SHRIMP AND SCALLOP SALAD

1/4 pound scallops
1 tablespoon olive oil
1 teaspoon minced garlic
1/4 pound peeled shrimp
1/4 cup seeded, chopped
   tomato
8 pimento-stuffed olives,
   thinly sliced
1/2 small red onion, thinly
   sliced
1 tablespoon olive oil
1 tablespoon Sherry vinegar
1/8 teaspoon paprika
1/8 teaspoon sugar
1 small head Bibb lettuce
8 Romaine lettuce leaves

Cut scallops into halves crosswise. Heat 1 tablespoon olive oil with garlic in skillet until hot but not smoking. Add scallops and shrimp. Sauté for 2 minutes. Stir in tomato, olives and onion. Remove to large bowl. Combine remaining 1 tablespoon olive oil, vinegar, paprika and sugar in bowl; mix well. Cut Bibb lettuce and Romaine lettuce into julienne strips. Combine with dressing in salad bowl. Add seafood mixture; toss to mix. Garnish with parsley, shrimp and lemon wedges. Yield: 4 servings.

Approx Per Serving: Cal 129; Prot 10 g; Carbo 4 g; Fiber 1 g; T Fat 9 g; Chol 52 mg; Sod 279 mg.

Jannie Barrington
Jones High School
Jones, Oklahoma

CRUNCHY SHRIMP SALAD

1 4-ounce can tiny shrimp,
  rinsed, drained
1 cup chopped celery
1 cup grated carrot
1 15-ounce can juice-pack
  pineapple tidbits, drained
3 tablespoons light
  mayonnaise-type salad
  dressing
1 5-ounce can chow mein
  noodles

Combine shrimp, celery, carrot and pineapple in bowl; mix well. Add salad dressing; mix well. Chill, covered, until serving time. Add chow mein noodles; toss to mix. Yield: 6 servings.

Approx Per Serving: Cal 209; Prot 8 g;
Carbo 29 g; Fiber 3 g; T Fat 8 g;
Chol 37 mg; Sod 330 mg.

Janice F. Stripes, C.H.E.
West Valley High School
Spokane, Washington

SHRIMP AND ORANGE SALAD

2 cups fresh spinach, torn
2 cups fresh lettuce, torn
1/2 cup mandarin oranges
1 cup cooked shrimp
1/4 cup sautéed water
  chestnuts
1/2 cup chopped honey-
  roasted peanuts
2 hard-boiled eggs, sliced

Combine greens with mandarin oranges, shrimp and water chestnuts in bowl; mix well. Place on serving plates. Top with peanuts and eggs. Serve immediately with your choice of dressing. Yield: 4 servings.

Approx Per Serving: Cal 215; Prot 16 g;
Carbo 11 g; Fiber 4 g; T Fat 13 g;
Chol 162 mg; Sod 119 mg.

Broxie C. Stuckey
Gordo High School
Gordo, Alabama

SHRIMP AND RICE SALAD

1 6-ounce can shrimp
1 cup chopped celery
1 cup cooked rice
1 cup chopped cauliflower
1 medium onion, chopped
7 stuffed olives, chopped
1 green bell pepper, chopped
1/2 cup mayonnaise
1 tablespoon lemon juice

Combine all ingredients in bowl; mix well. Chill in refrigerator. Yield: 4 servings.

Approx Per Serving: Cal 343; Prot 13 g;
Carbo 21 g; Fiber 3 g; T Fat 24 g;
Chol 90 mg; Sod 424 mg.

Shalan J. Inmon
Slaton High School
Slaton, Texas

SHRIMP SALAD

6 chicken breasts, cooked
3 pounds peeled cooked
   shrimp
4 cups imitation crab meat
3 8-ounce cans pineapple
   tidbits
5 cups white seedless grapes
4 cups finely chopped celery
1 cup slivered almonds
Cooked Pineapple Dressing
   (page 116)

Cut chicken breasts into bite-sized pieces. Combine with shrimp, crab meat, pineapple, grapes, celery and almonds in salad bowl. Add Cooked Pineapple Dressing; toss gently to coat. Serve immediately. Yield: 12 servings.

Approx Per Serving: Cal 434; Prot 45 g;
Carbo 38 g; Fiber 3 g; T Fat 12 g;
Chol 282 mg; Sod 725 mg.

Beverley C. Cole
Smyth County Vocational School
Marion, Virginia

SHRIMP MOLD

1 envelope unflavored
   gelatin
1/4 cup cold water
1/2 cup condensed tomato
   soup
6 ounces cream cheese,
   softened
1 7-ounce can shrimp,
   chopped
1/2 cup finely chopped celery
1/4 cup chopped onion
1/2 cup mayonnaise
Juice of 1/2 lemon

Soften gelatin in cold water. Bring soup to a boil in saucepan. Add gelatin, stirring until dissolved. Remove from heat. Beat in cream cheese. Add shrimp; mix well. Add celery, onion, mayonnaise and lemon juice; mix well. Pour into oiled mold. Chill until firm. Unmold onto lettuce-lined serving plate. Serve with crackers. Yield: 4 servings.

Approx Per Serving: Cal 440; Prot 17 g;
Carbo 8 g; Fiber 1 g; T Fat 38 g;
Chol 149 mg; Sod 599 mg.

Linnie Sue Comerford
Lantana Middle School
Lantana, Florida

 Make croutons from stale French bread. Sauté bread cubes in garlic butter and place on baking sheet. Bake in 300-degree oven until dry. Store in glass container.

SHRIMP SEA BREEZE

2 pounds peeled cooked
  shrimp, chilled
2/3 cup chopped celery
1/4 cup thinly sliced green
  onions
2 tablespoons finely
  chopped chives
1 cup oil
1/2 cup chili sauce
3 tablespoons lemon juice
2 tablespoons horseradish
1 tablespoon prepared
  mustard
1/2 teaspoon paprika
Hot pepper sauce to taste
1/2 teaspoon salt

Combine shrimp, celery, green onions and chives in salad bowl; mix well. Mix oil, chili sauce, lemon juice, horseradish, mustard, paprika, hot pepper sauce and salt in bowl; mix well. Pour over shrimp mixture; toss to mix. Chill, covered, overnight or longer.
Yield: 6 servings.

Approx Per Serving: Cal 504; Prot 32 g; Carbo 8 g; Fiber 1 g; T Fat 38 g; Chol 295 mg; Sod 870 mg.

Luann Crownover
Chillicothe High School
Chillicothe, Texas

ORIENTAL SPINACH SALAD WITH TUNA

8 cups chopped spinach
2 cups sliced mushrooms
1 cup bean sprouts
1/2 cup sliced purple onion
2 6-ounce cans water-
  pack tuna, drained
1 11-ounce can mandarin
  oranges, drained
Rice Vinegar Dressing
  (page 122)
1 teaspoon sesame seed

Combine spinach, mushrooms, bean sprouts, onion, tuna and mandarin oranges in bowl; mix well. Add Rice Vinegar Dressing; toss to mix. Sprinkle with sesame seed. Yield: 6 servings.

Approx Per Serving: Cal 170; Prot 21 g; Carbo 16 g; Fiber 5 g; T Fat 4 g; Chol 32 mg; Sod 288 mg.

Lenore Hamilton
Naperville Central High School
Naperville, Illinois

CHICKEN NOODLE-TUNA SALAD

1 3-ounce package lemon
   gelatin
½ cup boiling water
1 10-ounce can chicken
   noodle soup
½ cup chopped pecans
½ cup chopped celery
½ cup whipped topping
½ cup mayonnaise
1 6-ounce can water-pack
   chunk light tuna

Dissolve gelatin in boiling water in large bowl. Add soup, pecans, celery, whipped topping and mayonnaise; mix well. Rinse tuna with warm water; drain well. Add to salad; mix well. Chill overnight or until firm. Yield: 6 servings.

Approx Per Serving: Cal 330; Prot 13 g; Carbo 20 g; Fiber 1 g; T Fat 23 g; Chol 30 mg; Sod 621 mg.

*Roberta Stepp
Irving High School
Irving, Texas*

TUNA RICE MIX-UP

1 cup Green Goddess salad
   dressing
3 cups hot cooked white rice
¼ cup minced onion
¼ cup raisins
2 6-ounce cans water-
   pack tuna, drained
⅔ cup sliced celery
¼ cup finely chopped green
   pepper
⅓ cup chopped chutney
¼ cup chopped parsley
1 4-ounce jar chopped
   pimentos
1 16-ounce can cling peach
   slices, drained
⅓ cup cashews

Combine salad dressing, hot rice, onion and raisins in bowl; mix well. Chill, covered, for several minutes. Add tuna, celery, green pepper, chutney, parsley and pimentos; mix well. Chill until serving time. Spoon onto lettuce-lined serving plate. Arrange peach slices in starburst around edge; sprinkle with cashews.
Yield: 4 servings.

Approx Per Serving: Cal 670; Prot 33 g; Carbo 72 g; Fiber 5 g; T Fat 29 g; Chol 71 mg; Sod 663 mg.

*Janice F. Stripes, C.H.E.
West Valley High School
Spokane, Washington*

VIVA TUNA SPINACH SALAD

4 medium flour tortillas
2 medium tomatoes, chopped
4 green onions, chopped
8 fresh mushrooms, sliced
1   15-ounce can pinto beans,
    rinsed, drained
1 cup shredded low-fat
    Cheddar cheese
1   7-ounce can water-pack
    tuna, drained, flaked
2 bunches fresh spinach
½ cup light red wine and
    vinegar salad dressing

Cut tortillas into strips or wedges; place on baking sheet. Bake at 400 degrees for 3 to 5 minutes or until crisp. Combine tomatoes, green onions, mushrooms, pinto beans and cheese in large salad bowl. Add tuna; toss lightly. Add spinach and salad dressing; toss to coat well. Serve with crisp tortillas. May substitute salmon for tuna if preferred. Yield: 4 servings.

Approx Per Serving: Cal 446; Prot 37 g;
Carbo 56 g; Fiber 17 g; T Fat 9 g;
Chol 43 mg; Sod 516 mg.

Claudia Hall
Kasther Intermediate School
Fresno, California

TURKEY TACO SALAD

2 cups shredded sharp
    Cheddar cheese
1 head lettuce, coarsely
    chopped
3 tomatoes, coarsely chopped
1 avocado, coarsely chopped
3 to 5 green onions, chopped
1   16-ounce can kidney
    beans, drained
1   8-ounce bottle of Catalina
    dressing
2 tablespoons jalapeño chili
    relish
1 pound ground turkey
1   10-ounce package tortilla
    chips, crushed

Combine cheese, lettuce, tomatoes, avocado, green onions, beans, dressing and chili relish in bowl; mix well. Brown turkey in skillet, stirring frequently; drain. Add turkey and tortilla chips to salad just before serving. Yield: 6 servings.

Approx Per Serving: Cal 867; Prot 37 g;
Carbo 56 g; Fiber 13 g; T Fat 57 g;
Chol 112 mg; Sod 915 mg.

Judy Wenger
Shawnee Mission North High School
Shawnee Mission, Kansas

Salads Salads Salads Salads Salads
Salads Salads Salads Salads Salads
Salads Salads Salads Salads Salads
Salads Salads Salads Salads Salads

BUBBLY AMBROSIA

1 20-ounce can pineapple
  chunks, drained
2 large bananas, sliced
Sections of 3 large oranges
1 cup seedless grapes
1 3-ounce can flaked
  coconut
1 cup 7-Up
1 4-ounce jar maraschino
  cherries

Combine pineapple, bananas, oranges, grapes and 1 cup coconut in bowl; mix well. Chill until serving time. Spoon fruit mixture into individual bowls. Spoon 2 tablespoons 7-Up over top of each serving; sprinkle with remaining coconut. Garnish each serving with maraschino cherry. Yield: 8 servings.

Approx Per Serving: Cal 175; Prot 2 g; Carbo 37 g; Fiber 4 g; T Fat 4 g; Chol 0 mg; Sod 17 mg.

Brenda Kirby
Celina High School
Celina, Tennessee

LOW-CALORIE AMBROSIA

2 cups plain yogurt
4 envelopes artificial
  sweetener
1 teaspoon coconut extract
1 12-ounce can low-calorie
  fruit cocktail, drained
1/2 cup drained low-calorie
  mandarin oranges
1/2 cup drained low-calorie
  crushed pineapple
2 ounces shredded coconut

Combine yogurt, artificial sweetener and coconut extract in bowl; mix well. Add fruit cocktail, mandarin oranges and crushed pineapple; mix well. Chill until serving time. Sprinkle with coconut. Yield: 2 servings.

Approx Per Serving: Cal 426; Prot 14 g; Carbo 68 g; Fiber 7 g; T Fat 13 g; Chol 14 mg; Sod 242 mg.

Deborah Trust
South Meadow School
Peterborough, New Hampshire

 Use lemon-water to prevent fruits and vegetables from turning dark. When cutting up fruits and vegetables for salads, slice them into a mixture of 1/4 cup lemon juice and 4 cups cold water. Drain when ready to use.

APRICOT SALAD

1   6-ounce package apricot
    gelatin
1   20-ounce can crushed
    pineapple
2 cups buttermilk
8 ounces whipped topping
1 cup chopped pecans

Combine gelatin and crushed pineapple in saucepan. Bring to a boil, stirring until gelatin dissolves. Cool. Combine pineapple mixture and buttermilk in mixer bowl. Beat at high speed until well mixed. Fold in whipped topping and pecans. Spoon into serving bowl. Chill until set. Yield: 8 servings.

Approx Per Serving: Cal 348; Prot 6 g; Carbo 45 g; Fiber 2 g; T Fat 18 g; Chol 2 mg; Sod 140 mg.

Diane Sutton
Caddo Hills High School
Norman, Arkansas

PINEAPPLE AND APRICOT SALAD

2   3-ounce packages orange
    gelatin
1 cup boiling water
1½ cups cold water
1 cup pineapple-apricot juice
1   16-ounce can crushed
    pineapple, drained
1   16-ounce can apricots,
    drained, quartered
1 cup chopped pecans
½ cup sugar
3 tablespoons flour
1 egg, beaten
1 cup pineapple-apricot juice
2 tablespoons margarine
1 cup whipping cream,
    whipped
½ cup shredded Cheddar
    cheese

Dissolve gelatin in boiling water in bowl. Add cold water and 1 cup pineapple-apricot juice. Chill until partially set. Add pineapple, apricots and pecans. Pour into 9x9-inch dish. Chill until firm. Combine sugar, flour and egg in saucepan; mix well. Stir in remaining 1 cup pineapple-apricot juice and margarine. Cook over low heat until thickened, stirring constantly. Let stand until cool. Fold in whipped cream. Spread over congealed layer. Sprinkle with cheese. Chill in refrigerator. Yield: 6 servings.

Approx Per Serving: Cal 672; Prot 10 g; Carbo 84 g; Fiber 3 g; T Fat 36 g; Chol 100 mg; Sod 226 mg.

Janice Dowlearn
DeSoto High School
DeSoto, Texas

SWEET AND CREAMY APRICOT MOLD

1 6-ounce package apricot
   gelatin
2/3 cup sugar
2/3 cup water
1 20-ounce can crushed
   pineapple
2 3-ounce jars baby food
   strained apricots
1 12-ounce can evaporated
   milk, chilled
8 ounces cream cheese,
   softened
1/2 cup chopped pecans

Combine gelatin, sugar and water in saucepan. Bring to a boil, stirring until gelatin and sugar are dissolved. Remove from heat. Add undrained pineapple and apricots; mix well. Chill until partially set. Combine evaporated milk and cream cheese in mixer bowl. Beat until smooth and creamy. Fold in gelatin mixture and pecans. Pour into lightly-oiled 8-cup mold. Chill until set. Yield: 8 servings.

*Approx Per Serving: Cal 414; Prot 8 g;
Carbo 58 g; Fiber 2 g; T Fat 18 g;
Chol 43 mg; Sod 199 mg.*

Sarah Gomez
Halton High School
Fort Worth, Texas

BANANA AND DATE SALAD

1 20-ounce can pineapple
   tidbits
1/2 cup sugar
1 tablespoon flour
1 egg, slightly beaten
1 tablespoon lemon juice
1/8 teaspoon salt
4 large bananas, sliced
1 8-ounce package chopped
   dates

Drain pineapple, reserving juice. Combine pineapple juice, sugar, flour, egg, lemon juice and salt in saucepan; mix well. Cook until thickened, stirring constantly. Cool. Combine pineapple, bananas and dates in salad bowl; mix well. Add cooled dressing; mix gently. Yield: 8 servings.

*Approx Per Serving: Cal 248; Prot 2 g;
Carbo 62 g; Fiber 4 g; T Fat 1 g;
Chol 27 mg; Sod 44 mg.*

Carol Woods
Midway High School
Hewitt, Texas

 *For a quick snack, cut a kiwifruit in half from the blossom end to
the stem end—then eat with a teaspoon!*

FROZEN BANANA SALAD

1 7-ounce jar marshmallow
  creme
2 cups drained crushed
  pineapple
2 to 4 tablespoons pineapple
  juice
4 bananas, mashed
16 ounces creamed cottage
  cheese
1 cup whipped topping
1/2 cup chopped pecans

Combine marshmallow creme, pineapple, pineapple juice, bananas and cottage cheese in bowl; mix well. Fold in whipped topping and pecans. Pour into two 16-ounce coffee cans. Cover with plastic wrap. Freeze until firm. Unmold onto serving plate; cut into slices. May also be frozen in muffin cups or 9x13-inch glass dish. Yield: 12 servings.

Approx Per Serving: Cal 224; Prot 6 g;
Carbo 33 g; Fiber 2 g; T Fat 8 g;
Chol 6 mg; Sod 167 mg.

Penny M. Norman
Elbert County Comprehensive High School
Elberton, Georgia

BLUEBERRY GELATIN SALAD

1 16-ounce can crushed
  pineapple
1 3-ounce package orange
  gelatin
1 6-ounce package
  strawberry gelatin
2 cups boiling water
1 21-ounce can blueberry
  pie filling
1 11/2-ounce package
  whipped topping mix
1/2 cup milk

Drain pineapple, reserving juice. Add enough water to reserved pineapple juice to measure 3/4 cup. Dissolve gelatins in boiling water in bowl. Add pineapple juice, pineapple and pie filling; mix well. Reserve 11/2 cups. Pour remaining gelatin mixture into 9x13-inch glass dish. Chill until set. Chill reserved gelatin mixture until thickened. Prepare whipped topping with milk using package directions. Fold into thickened gelatin. Spread over congealed layer. Chill until set. Yield: 12 servings.

Approx Per Serving: Cal 182; Prot 3 g;
Carbo 41 g; Fiber 1 g; T Fat 2 g;
Chol 1 mg; Sod 91 mg.

Lynn Melton
Slaton High School
Slaton, Texas

CHERRY AND BLUEBERRY SALAD

1 16-ounce can blueberries
1 15-ounce can crushed
   pineapple
1 6-ounce package black
   cherry gelatin
8 ounces cream cheese,
   softened
1 cup sour cream
1/4 cup sugar
1 cup finely chopped pecans

Drain blueberries and pineapple, reserving juice. Add enough water to juice to measure 2 cups. Bring juice to a boil in saucepan. Stir in gelatin until dissolved. Pour into 9x12-inch glass dish. Chill until partially set. Add blueberries and pineapple; mix well. Chill until set. Combine cream cheese, sour cream and sugar in bowl; mix well. Stir in pecans. Spread over congealed salad. Chill until firm. Yield: 12 servings.

Approx Per Serving: Cal 303; Prot 4 g;
Carbo 35 g; Fiber 2 g; T Fat 18 g;
Chol 29 mg; Sod 113 mg.

Dorothy Cunningham
Ransom Middle School
Cantonment, Florida

RASPBERRY AND BLUEBERRY SALAD

1 6-ounce package
   raspberry gelatin
1 cup boiling water
1 8-ounce can crushed
   pineapple
1 21-ounce can blueberry
   pie filling
1 cup sour cream
8 ounces cream cheese,
   softened
1/3 cup sugar
1 cup chopped pecans

Dissolve gelatin in boiling water in bowl. Add undrained pineapple and pie filling; mix well. Pour into 9x13-inch glass dish. Chill until set. Combine sour cream, cream cheese and sugar in bowl; mix well. Stir in pecans. Spread over congealed gelatin. Garnish with additional chopped pecans. Chill until serving time.
Yield: 12 servings.

Approx Per Serving: Cal 309; Prot 4 g;
Carbo 37 g; Fiber 1 g; T Fat 17 g;
Chol 29 mg; Sod 126 mg.

Nancy Moody
Pocahontas High School
Pocahontas, Arkansas

 Use canned rather than fresh pineapple in a gelatin salad. The enzymes in the fresh pineapple keep the gelatin from setting.

BUTTERMILK SALAD

1 cup water
1 6-ounce package orange
   gelatin
1 8-ounce can crushed
   pineapple
2 cups buttermilk
12 ounces whipped topping

Combine water, orange gelatin and pineapple in saucepan. Bring to a boil, stirring until gelatin dissolves. Cool. Add buttermilk and whipped topping. Pour into mold. Chill until set. Yield: 10 servings.

*Approx Per Serving: Cal 209; Prot 4 g;
Carbo 30 g; Fiber <1 g; T Fat 9 g;
Chol 2 mg; Sod 114 mg.*

*Marvelyn Smith
Heritage High School
Conyers, Georgia*

CHAMPAGNE SALAD

8 ounces cream cheese,
   softened
3/4 cup sugar
1 10-ounce package frozen
   strawberries, thawed,
   drained
1 20-ounce can crushed
   pineapple, drained
2 bananas, mashed
1 cup chopped English
   walnuts
9 ounces whipped topping

Combine cream cheese and sugar in bowl; mix well. Stir in next 4 ingredients. Fold in whipped topping. Spoon into 9x13-inch glass dish. Freeze until firm. Let stand at room temperature for 10 minutes before serving. Yield: 12 servings.

*Approx Per Serving: Cal 296; Prot 4 g;
Carbo 33 g; Fiber 2 g; T Fat 18 g;
Chol 21 mg; Sod 64 mg.*

*Melissa Helbig
Republic High School
Republic, Missouri*

CHERRY SALAD

1 21-ounce can cherry pie
   filling
1 8-ounce can crushed
   pineapple, drained
1 1/2 cups miniature
   marshmallows
12 ounces whipped topping
1 cup chopped pecans
3 or 4 drops of red food
   coloring

Combine pie filling, pineapple and marshmallows in bowl; mix well. Fold in whipped topping, pecans and food coloring. Yield: 6 servings.

*Approx Per Serving: Cal 472; Prot 3 g;
Carbo 58 g; Fiber 3 g; T Fat 28 g;
Chol 0 mg; Sod 57 mg.*

*Kathy Worrell
Udall High School
Udall, Kansas*

CHERRY FRUIT SALAD

2 red apples, chopped
2 golden apples, chopped
4 bananas, sliced
2 pears, chopped
2 mangos, chopped
1   11-ounce can mandarin
    oranges, drained
1   16-ounce can pineapple
    chunks, drained
1 cup chopped pecans
1   21-ounce can cherry pie
    filling

Combine apples, bananas, pears, mangos, mandarin oranges, pineapple and pecans in large glass bowl; mix well. Add pie filling; mix well. Chill overnight. May immerse apples, bananas, pears and mangos in lemon water to prevent browning. Drain well. Yield: 10 servings.

Approx Per Serving: Cal 299; Prot 2 g;
Carbo 59 g; Fiber 7 g; T Fat 9 g;
Chol 0 mg; Sod 22 mg.

Dorothy L. Jones
Eula Independent School District
Clyde, Texas

CHERRY SNOWBALL RING MOLD

1   6-ounce package cherry
    gelatin
2 cups boiling water
1   29-ounce can dark sweet
    cherries
1   29-ounce can crushed
    pineapple
8 ounces cream cheese,
    softened
2/3 cup chopped pecans

Dissolve gelatin in boiling water in bowl. Drain cherries and pineapple, reserving 1 2/3 cups mixed juices. Add reserved juices to gelatin. Chill until partially set. Shape cream cheese into 24 small balls; roll in chopped pecans. Place in 8-inch ring mold. Add cherries and pineapple to gelatin. Spoon gelatin over cream cheese balls. Chill until firm. Unmold onto lettuce-lined salad plate. Garnish with mayonnaise.
Yield: 6 servings.

Approx Per Serving: Cal 1021; Prot 16 g;
Carbo 85 g; Fiber 3 g; T Fat 70 g;
Chol 240 mg; Sod 1884 mg.

Lou Ann Tucker
Waldron High School
Waldron, Arkansas

 Use muffin tins for individual gelatin molds.

PRETTY PINK SALAD

1 21-ounce can cherry pie
   filling
1 14-ounce can sweetened
   condensed milk, chilled
2 cups miniature
   marshmallows
1 20-ounce can crushed
   pineapple, drained
8 ounces whipped topping

Combine pie filling, condensed milk, marshmallows and pineapple in large bowl; mix well. Fold in whipped topping. Spoon into serving bowl. Chill for 2 hours or longer. Yield: 15 servings.

Approx Per Serving: Cal 214; Prot 3 g;
Carbo 39 g; Fiber 1 g; T Fat 6 g;
Chol 9 mg; Sod 56 mg.

Holly Martin
Webster City High School
Webster City, Iowa

MERRY CRANBERRY FREEZE

3 cups finely chopped
   cranberries
1½ cups sugar
8 ounces cream cheese,
   softened
1 8-ounce can crushed
   pineapple, drained
½ cup chopped walnuts
1 cup whipping cream,
   whipped

Combine cranberries and sugar in bowl; mix well. Let stand for 10 minutes or until sugar dissolves, stirring frequently. Beat cream cheese in mixer bowl. Add pineapple; mix well. Stir in walnuts and cranberry mixture. Fold in whipped cream. Spoon into a lightly-oiled 7½-cup mold. Freeze until firm. May freeze in paper-lined muffin cups if desired. Yield: 15 servings.

Approx Per Serving: Cal 227; Prot 2 g;
Carbo 26 g; Fiber 1 g; T Fat 14 g;
Chol 38 mg; Sod 52 mg.

Margie Pope
La Fayette High School
La Fayette, Georgia

 During the holidays your refrigerator door is opened so often that congealed salads have a problem firming. Make these salads one day earlier than usual.

CRAN-RASPBERRY RING

1 3-ounce package
  raspberry gelatin
1 3-ounce package lemon
  gelatin
2 cups boiling water
1 10-ounce package frozen
  raspberries
1 14-ounce jar cranberry-
  orange relish
1 11-ounce can mandarin
  oranges, drained
1 7-ounce bottle of
  lemon-lime soda

Dissolve raspberry gelatin and lemon gelatin in boiling water in bowl. Add frozen raspberries, stirring to break apart. Add relish. Reserve several mandarin orange slices for garnish. Add remaining mandarin oranges; mix well. Chill until partially set. Add lemon-lime soda, stirring gently. Pour into 6-cup ring mold or 9x13-inch glass dish. Chill until set. Garnish with lettuce and reserved mandarin orange slices.
Yield: 8 servings.

Approx Per Serving: Cal 237; Prot 3 g; Carbo 60 g; Fiber 4 g; T Fat <1 g; Chol 0 mg; Sod 89 mg.

Nancy P. Nicol
Omaha South High School
Omaha, Nebraska

FRESH CRANBERRY SALAD

1 6-ounce package
  raspberry gelatin
1 cup sugar
1 cup boiling water
1/2 cup cold water
2 cups chopped fresh
  cranberries
1 teaspoon grated orange rind
Sections of 1 orange
1 cup chopped pecans

Dissolve gelatin and sugar in boiling water in bowl. Add cold water, cranberries, orange rind, orange sections and pecans; mix well. Chill until partially set. Pour into 8x8-inch glass dish. Chill until firm. Yield: 12 servings.

Approx Per Serving: Cal 196; Prot 2 g; Carbo 34 g; Fiber 2 g; T Fat 7 g; Chol 0 mg; Sod 46 mg.

Mitzi B. Hardin
Calhoun City High School
Calhoun City, Mississippi

FROZEN CRANBERRY SALAD

1 20-ounce can crushed
   pineapple, drained
¼ cup lemon juice
1 14-ounce can sweetened
   condensed milk
1 16-ounce can whole-berry
   cranberry sauce
½ cup chopped pecans
8 ounces whipped topping

Combine pineapple, lemon juice, condensed milk, cranberry sauce and pecans in bowl; mix well. Fold in whipped topping. Spoon into 9x13-inch dish. Cover with plastic wrap. Freeze until firm. Yield: 12 servings.

Approx Per Serving: Cal 282; Prot 4 g;
Carbo 45 g; Fiber 2 g; T Fat 11 g;
Chol 11 mg; Sod 58 mg.

Susan McGregor
Yukon Middle High School
Yukon, Oklahoma

NUTTY CRANBERRY AND FRUIT GELATIN

1 6-ounce package lemon
   gelatin
1 16-ounce can whole-berry
   cranberry sauce
1 cup chopped walnuts
1 11-ounce can mandarin
   oranges, drained
1 8-ounce can crushed
   pineapple
2 cups 7-Up

Combine gelatin and cranberry sauce in saucepan. Bring to a boil over medium heat, stirring until gelatin is dissolved. Remove from heat. Stir in walnuts, oranges, undrained pineapple and 7-Up. Let stand until fizzing stops. Pour into oiled 5-cup mold. Chill until set. Yield: 8 servings.

Approx Per Serving: Cal 332; Prot 5 g;
Carbo 62 g; Fiber 3 g; T Fat 9 g;
Chol 0 mg; Sod 95 mg.

Nancy Alexander
Unioto High School
Chillicothe, Ohio

 When making your favorite gelatin, use the juice from a can of fruit instead of water to add extra flavor and zip. Or use ginger ale instead of the cold water to add pizzazz.

CRANBERRY SALAD

1 16-ounce package
  cranberries, ground
1 cup sugar
1 10-ounce package
  miniature marshmallows
2 cups ground apples
2 cups whipping cream,
  whipped
1/2 cup chopped walnuts

Combine cranberries and sugar in bowl; mix well. Stir in marshmallows. Chill overnight. Add apples; mix well. Fold in whipped cream and walnuts. Spoon into serving bowl. Yield: 12 servings.

Approx Per Serving: Cal 337; Prot 2 g; Carbo 45 g; Fiber 2 g; T Fat 18 g; Chol 54 mg; Sod 37 mg.

Judy Wenger
Shawnee Mission North High School
Shawnee Mission, Kansas

TASTY CRANBERRY SALAD

1 20-ounce can crushed
  pineapple
1 6-ounce package cherry
  gelatin
3/4 cup sugar
2 cups boiling water
1/2 cup cold water
1 or 2 tablespoons lemon
  juice
1 1/2 cups ground fresh
  cranberries
1 small orange, ground
1 cup chopped celery
1/2 cup chopped walnuts

Drain pineapple, reserving juice. Dissolve gelatin and sugar in boiling water in bowl. Stir in reserved pineapple juice, 1/2 cup cold water and lemon juice. Chill until partially set. Add pineapple, cranberries, orange, celery and walnuts; mix well. Spoon into mold. Chill until firm. Unmold onto serving plate. Garnish with softened cream cheese. Yield: 12 servings.

Approx Per Serving: Cal 183; Prot 2 g; Carbo 39 g; Fiber 2 g; T Fat 3 g; Chol 0 mg; Sod 55 mg.

Joette Tribble
Martins Mill Independent School District
Ben Wheeler, Texas

FIVE-CUP SALAD

1 16-ounce can pineapple
   chunks
1 banana
1 11-ounce can mandarin
   oranges, drained
1 cup miniature
   marshmallows
¹/₂ cup coconut
1 cup sour cream

Drain pineapple, reserving juice. Cut banana into slices. Add banana to reserved pineapple juice, stirring to coat; drain. Combine with pineapple and mandarin oranges in 2-quart bowl. Add marshmallows, coconut and sour cream; mix well. Yield: 8 servings.

Approx Per Serving: Cal 187; Prot 2 g;
Carbo 30 g; Fiber 2 g; T Fat 8 g;
Chol 13 mg; Sod 26 mg.
Nutritional information includes
entire amount of reserved pineapple juice.

Kathy Thomas
Chickasha Junior High School
Chickasha, Oklahoma

GOOSEBERRY SALAD

1 3-ounce package lemon
   gelatin
1 3-ounce package lime
   gelatin
1 cup boiling water
1 16-ounce can gooseberries
1 cup sugar
1 cup chopped celery
1 cup shredded Cheddar
   cheese
1 cup chopped pecans

Dissolve lemon gelatin and lime gelatin in boiling water in bowl. Cool. Combine gooseberries and sugar in bowl. Let stand for 1 hour. Add celery, cheese and pecans to gooseberries; mix gently. Fold into gelatin mixture. Spoon into serving bowl. Chill until firm. This salad is rather tart. Yield: 10 servings.

Approx Per Serving: Cal 300; Prot 6 g;
Carbo 46 g; Fiber 2 g; T Fat 12 g;
Chol 12 mg; Sod 136 mg.

Judy Adler
Snyder High School
Snyder, Oklahoma

 In warm weather add a package of unflavored gelatin to keep a gelatin salad from weeping or melting so rapidly.

FROZEN LIME MINT SALAD

1 20-ounce can crushed
  pineapple
1 3-ounce package lime
  gelatin
1 6-ounce package
  miniature marshmallows
1 cup crushed butter mints
4 ounces whipped topping

Combine undrained pineapple, lime gelatin, marshmallows and butter mints in bowl; mix well. Chill for several hours to soften marshmallows. Fold in whipped topping. Spoon into paper-lined muffin cups. Cover with plastic wrap. Freeze until firm. Peel off paper liners before serving. Yield: 12 servings.

Approx Per Serving: Cal 174; Prot 2 g; Carbo 34 g; Fiber 1 g; T Fat 4 g; Chol 3 mg; Sod 50 mg.

Beverly Searcy
Simon Kenton High School
Independence, Kentucky

LIME GELATIN SALAD

1 6-ounce package lime
  gelatin
2 cups boiling water
1 cup crushed pineapple
3 bananas, mashed
1 cup whipped topping

Dissolve gelatin in boiling water in bowl. Cool. Add pineapple and bananas; mix well. Pour half the gelatin mixture into mold. Chill until firm. Spread whipped topping over congealed layer. Spoon remaining gelatin mixture over whipped topping. Chill until firm. Yield: 6 servings.

Approx Per Serving: Cal 231; Prot 4 g; Carbo 50 g; Fiber 2 g; T Fat 3 g; Chol 0 mg; Sod 94 mg.

Peggy Chambers
Tushka High School
Atoka, Oklahoma

To serve fresh pineapple, cut into quarters lengthwise; remove core. Cut out pineapple next to peel, reserving shells. Cut pineapple into wedge chunks and serve in reserved shells.

LIME WALNUT SALAD

1 3-ounce package lime
   gelatin
1 cup boiling water
1 20-ounce can crushed
   pineapple, drained
1 cup cottage cheese
1/2 cup sliced celery
1/2 cup chopped walnuts

Dissolve gelatin in boiling water in bowl. Add pineapple, cottage cheese, celery and walnuts; mix well. Pour into serving dish. Chill until firm. May top congealed salad with mixture of 3 ounces softened cream cheese, 1 tablespoon mayonnaise and 1 tablespoon lemon juice. Yield: 8 servings.

Approx Per Serving: Cal 152; Prot 6 g; Carbo 21 g; Fiber 1 g; T Fat 6 g; Chol 4 mg; Sod 148 mg.

Jan Arthur
Union Public School
Union, Mississippi

CHRISTMAS RAINBOW SALAD

1 3-ounce package lime
   gelatin
1 cup boiling water
1 cup cold water
1 3-ounce package lemon
   gelatin
2 cups boiling water
3 ounces cream cheese,
   softened
1 cup crushed pineapple
2 cups miniature
   marshmallows
1/2 cup whipping cream,
   whipped
1 3-ounce package
   strawberry gelatin
1 cup boiling water
1 cup cold water

Dissolve lime gelatin in 1 cup boiling water in bowl. Add 1 cup cold water; mix well. Pour into 10x10-inch glass dish. Chill until firm. Dissolve lemon gelatin in 2 cups boiling water. Cool. Add cream cheese, pineapple and marshmallows; mix well. Fold in whipped cream. Pour over congealed lime gelatin layer. Chill until firm. Dissolve strawberry gelatin in 1 cup boiling water. Add 1 cup cold water; mix well. Pour over congealed lemon gelatin layer. Chill until set. Yield: 9 servings.

Approx Per Serving: Cal 246; Prot 4 g; Carbo 42 g; Fiber <1 g; T Fat 8 g; Chol 28 mg; Sod 134 mg.

Arlene LaVoy
Columbia River High School
Vancouver, Washington

MELON SALAD

1 10-pound watermelon
1 small honeydew melon
3 cups cranberry juice
1 cup corn syrup
2 tablespoons lime juice
8 ounces cream cheese,
    softened
1/4 cup milk
3 tablespoons sugar
3 tablespoons lemon juice
3/4 teaspoon cardamom

Cut watermelon into basket shape. Scoop out melon; cut into bite-sized pieces. Cut honeydew melon into bite-sized pieces. Mix cranberry juice, corn syrup and lime juice in large bowl. Add melons. Marinate in refrigerator for 3 hours; drain. Combine cream cheese and milk in bowl; mix well. Add sugar, lemon juice and cardamom; mix well. Place melon cubes in melon basket. Serve with cardamom dressing. Yield: 20 servings.

Approx Per Serving: Cal 210; Prot 3 g; Carbo 43 g; Fiber 2 g; T Fat 5 g; Chol 13 mg; Sod 54 mg.

Marla Prusa
Clarkson Public High School
Clarkson, Nebraska

HEAVENLY ORANGE FLUFF

1 6-ounce package orange
    gelatin
2 cups boiling water
1 6-ounce can frozen orange
    juice concentrate
2 11-ounce cans mandarin
    oranges, drained
1 20-ounce can crushed
    pineapple
1 4-ounce package lemon
    instant pudding mix
1 cup milk
1/2 cup whipping cream,
    whipped

Dissolve gelatin in boiling water in bowl. Stir in orange juice concentrate. Cool. Add mandarin oranges and undrained pineapple. Pour into 9x13-inch dish. Chill until firm. Beat instant pudding and milk in bowl until thickened. Fold in whipped cream. Spread over congealed layer. Chill until serving time. Cut into squares. Serve on lettuce-lined salad plates. Yield: 12 servings.

Approx Per Serving: Cal 226; Prot 3 g; Carbo 46 g; Fiber 2 g; T Fat 5 g; Chol 16 mg; Sod 125 mg.

Debbie Bailey Smith
East Rutherford High School
Forest City, North Carolina

ORANGE FLUFF

10 ounces cottage cheese
6 ounces whipped topping
1 3-ounce package orange
   gelatin
1 11-ounce can mandarin
   oranges, drained

Combine cottage cheese and whipped topping in bowl. Add gelatin; mix well. Stir in mandarin oranges. Chill for several hours before serving. Yield: 6 servings.

Approx Per Serving: Cal 223; Prot 8 g;
Carbo 29 g; Fiber 1 g; T Fat 9 g;
Chol 7 mg; Sod 247 mg.

Anna Smith
Muscle Shoals High School
Muscle Shoals, Alabama

ORANGE FRUIT SALAD

1 3-ounce package orange
   gelatin
3/4 cup boiling water
3 ounces cream cheese,
   softened
1/2 10-ounce package
   miniature marshmallows
1 11-ounce can mandarin
   oranges, drained
1/2 cup evaporated milk
1/3 cup mayonnaise
1 teaspoon lemon juice
1/2 cup chopped pecans

Combine gelatin, water, cream cheese and marshmallows in saucepan. Cook over low heat, stirring until gelatin is dissolved. Pour into mixer bowl; beat well. Cool. Stir in mandarin oranges, evaporated milk, mayonnaise, lemon juice and pecans. Pour into 8x8-inch glass dish. Chill until firm. Yield: 8 servings.

Approx Per Serving: Cal 293; Prot 4 g;
Carbo 34 g; Fiber 1 g; T Fat 17 g;
Chol 22 mg; Sod 151 mg.

Lynne Bell
Hibriten High School
Lenoir, North Carolina

 Ice cubes may be used to replace part of the cold water in making gelatin salads so that the mixture gels faster.

ORANGE PRETZEL SALAD

2½ cups crushed pretzels
3 tablespoons brown sugar
¾ cup melted margarine
8 ounces cream cheese,
  softened
1 cup confectioners' sugar
9 ounces whipped topping
1   6-ounce package orange
  gelatin
1   11-ounce can mandarin
  oranges, drained

Combine pretzels, brown sugar and margarine in bowl; mix well. Press into 9x13-inch baking dish. Bake at 350 degrees for 10 minutes. Cool. Combine cream cheese and confectioners' sugar in bowl; mix well. Fold in whipped topping. Spread over cooled crust. Chill in refrigerator. Prepare gelatin using package directions. Pour over cream cheese layer. Chill until set. Arrange mandarin oranges over top. May substitute strawberry gelatin for orange gelatin and garnish with strawberries. Yield: 12 servings.

*Approx Per Serving: Cal 403; Prot 4 g;
Carbo 45 g; Fiber 1 g; T Fat 24 g;
Chol 21 mg; Sod 434 mg.*

*Martha Fields
Mitchell High School
Mitchell, Indiana*

ORANGE REFRIGERATOR SALAD

12 ounces small curd cottage
  cheese
1   3-ounce package orange
  gelatin
1   11-ounce can mandarin
  oranges, drained
1   8-ounce can crushed
  pineapple, drained
4 ounces whipped topping

Combine cottage cheese and gelatin in bowl; mix well. Add mandarin oranges and pineapple. Stir gently. Fold in whipped topping. Chill, covered, for 4 hours or longer. Yield: 4 servings.

*Approx Per Serving: Cal 334; Prot 14 g;
Carbo 48 g; Fiber 2 g; T Fat 11 g;
Chol 13 mg; Sod 424 mg.*

*Susan D. Sohn
Glenelg High School
Glenelg, Maryland*

ORANGE SHERBET CONGEALED SALAD

2 3-ounce packages orange
  gelatin
4 cups boiling water
1 quart orange sherbet,
  softened
1 8-ounce can pineapple
  chunks, drained
1 8-ounce can mandarin
  oranges, drained
1½ cups miniature
  marshmallows
1 cup coconut
1 cup chopped pecans
1 cup sour cream

Dissolve gelatin in boiling water. Stir in sherbet. Pour into round ring mold. Chill overnight until set. Combine pineapple, mandarin oranges, marshmallows, coconut, pecans and sour cream in bowl; mix well. Unmold gelatin onto serving plate. Fill center of ring with fruit mixture. May spoon additional fruit mixture around outside of ring if desired. Yield: 8 servings.

*Approx Per Serving: Cal 476; Prot 6 g;
Carbo 71 g; Fiber 3 g; T Fat 21 g;
Chol 20 mg; Sod 161 mg.*

*Donna Stroupe
Wheeler High School
Wheeler, Mississippi*

PEACH GELATIN SALAD

1 6-ounce package peach
  gelatin
2 cups boiling water
2 cups miniature
  marshmallows
1 8-ounce can crushed
  pineapple
8 ounces cream cheese,
  softened
1 cup chopped pecans
8 ounces whipped topping

Dissolve gelatin in boiling water in bowl. Add marshmallows, stirring until partially melted. Mix pineapple and cream cheese in bowl. Fold in pecans and whipped topping. Add to gelatin mixture; mix gently. Pour into 9x12-inch glass dish. Chill until set. Yield: 8 servings.

*Approx Per Serving: Cal 434; Prot 6 g;
Carbo 46 g; Fiber 1 g; T Fat 27 g;
Chol 31 mg; Sod 172 mg.*

*Janice Sapp
Claxton High School
Claxton, Georgia*

 *To unmold gelatin salads easily, dip mold in warm water for a few
seconds. Tilt slightly to ease gelatin away from one side.*

PEAR SALAD

1 16-ounce can pears
1 3-ounce package lemon
  gelatin
8 ounces cream cheese,
  softened
2 cups whipped topping

Drain pears, reserving juice. Chop enough pears to measure 1 cup. Add enough water to reserved pear juice to measure 1½ cups. Combine pear juice and gelatin in saucepan. Bring to a boil, stirring to dissolve gelatin. Remove from heat. Add cream cheese, stirring until melted. Pour into bowl. Chill until partially set. Fold in whipped topping and chopped pears. Spoon into mold. Chill until set. Yield: 8 servings.

Approx Per Serving: Cal 240; Prot 3 g;
Carbo 25 g; Fiber 1 g; T Fat 15 g;
Chol 31 mg; Sod 125 mg.

Jan Knuth
Southeast High School
Wichita, Kansas

BEST GREEN SALAD

16 ounces whipped topping
1 3-ounce package lime
  gelatin
1 8-ounce can crushed
  pineapple, drained
8 ounces cottage cheese
½ cup chopped pecans

Combine whipped topping and gelatin in bowl; mix well. Add pineapple, cottage cheese and pecans; mix well. Spoon into serving dish. Chill for 1 hour or longer. Yield: 8 servings.

Approx Per Serving: Cal 313; Prot 6 g;
Carbo 28 g; Fiber 1 g; T Fat 21 g;
Chol 4 mg; Sod 163 mg.

Sherie Mauney
Walnut Attendance Center
Walnut, Mississippi

 A fresh pineapple is ready to cut when top middle leaves pull out easily, it has a sweet smell at base, starts turning golden color or pineapple design looses its indentation. A pineapple will have a sweet flavor if turned upside-down one to two days before cutting.

PINEAPPLE-CHEESE SALAD

1   20-ounce can pineapple
     tidbits
1/2 cup sugar
1 egg, beaten
4 1/2 teaspoons flour
8 ounces Velveeta cheese
1/4 cup chopped pecans
1 cup miniature
     marshmallows

Drain pineapple, reserving juice. Combine reserved juice, sugar, egg and flour in saucepan. Cook over medium heat until thickened, stirring constantly. Chill in refrigerator. Cut cheese into bite-sized pieces. Combine with pineapple, pecans and marshmallows in bowl. Fold in dressing. Chill until serving time. This is a very good salad to serve with ham. Yield: 6 servings.

Approx Per Serving: Cal 362; Prot 11 g;
Carbo 46 g; Fiber 1 g; T Fat 16 g;
Chol 71 mg; Sod 562 mg.

Judy Graham
Pioneer High School
Royal Center, Indiana

SAWDUST SALAD

1   3-ounce package orange
     gelatin
1   3-ounce package lemon
     gelatin
2 cups boiling water
1 1/2 cups cold water
1   20-ounce can crushed
     pineapple
2 or 3 bananas, sliced
2 cups miniature
     marshmallows
2 eggs, beaten
1/2 cup sugar
1 teaspoon vanilla extract
2 tablespoons flour
1 cup whipping cream
8 ounces cream cheese,
     softened
2 cups shredded Cheddar
     cheese

Dissolve orange gelatin and lemon gelatin in boiling water in bowl. Add cold water; mix well. Chill until partially set. Drain pineapple, reserving 1 cup juice. Add pineapple and bananas to gelatin; mix well. Pour into 9x13-inch glass dish. Sprinkle with marshmallows. Chill until set. Combine reserved pineapple juice, eggs, sugar, vanilla and flour in saucepan. Cook until thickened, stirring constantly. Cool. Spread over marshmallow layer. Beat whipping cream and cream cheese in bowl until thick and creamy. Spread over salad. Top with Cheddar cheese. Chill overnight. Yield: 12 servings.

Approx Per Serving: Cal 407; Prot 10 g;
Carbo 47 g; Fiber 1 g; T Fat 21 g;
Chol 103 mg; Sod 246 mg.

Linda Sahnow
Lebanon High School
Lebanon, Oregon

FRUIT SALAD

1   3-ounce package lemon
    gelatin
1 cup boiling water
1   8-ounce can crushed
    pineapple
1/4 cup cold water
16 ounces cottage cheese
96 colored miniature
    marshmallows
8 ounces whipped topping

Dissolve gelatin in boiling water in bowl. Drain pineapple, reserving 3/4 cup juice. Add reserved juice and cold water to gelatin; mix well. Chill until partially set. Add pineapple, cottage cheese and marshmallows; mix well. Fold in whipped topping. Chill until set.
Yield: 12 servings.

Approx Per Serving: Cal 134; Prot 6 g;
Carbo 19 g; Fiber <1 g; T Fat 4 g;
Chol 7 mg; Sod 193 mg.

Marie Fiorenza
Adirondack K-8
Boonville, New York

PINEAPPLE SALAD

1   20-ounce can pineapple
    chunks
1 egg, beaten
1 tablespoon flour
3 tablespoons sugar
1/2 cup miniature
    marshmallows
1/2 cup Velveeta cheese cubes
1/4 cup chopped pecans

Drain pineapple, reserving juice. Combine reserved pineapple juice, egg, flour and sugar in saucepan; mix well. Cook over medium heat until thickened, stirring constantly. Cool. Combine cooled dressing, marshmallows, cheese cubes, pecans and pineapple in serving bowl; mix well. Chill until serving time.
Yield: 6 servings.

Approx Per Serving: Cal 199; Prot 4 g;
Carbo 31 g; Fiber 1 g; T Fat 7 g;
Chol 45 mg; Sod 152 mg.

Jane Asberry
Greenville High School
Greenville, Texas

 For a great quick dressing for fruit, mix 2 tablespoons whipped topping and 2 tablespoons sour cream.

BERRY SALAD

1 3-ounce package
   raspberry gelatin
1 cup boiling water
2 cups red raspberries
1/2 cup applesauce

Dissolve gelatin in boiling water in bowl. Stir in raspberries and applesauce. Spoon into mold or dish. Chill until firm. Serve with whipped topping or sweetened whipped cream. Yield: 6 servings.

Approx Per Serving: Cal 81; Prot 2 g; Carbo 20 g; Fiber 3 g; T Fat <1 g; Chol 0 mg; Sod 45 mg.

*Martha Fields
Mitchell High School
Mitchell, Indiana*

RASPBERRIES AND CREAM SALAD

1 3-ounce package
   raspberry gelatin
1 1/3 cups boiling water
1 10-ounce package frozen
   raspberries
1 3-ounce package lemon
   gelatin
2 cups boiling water
4 cups miniature
   marshmallows
8 ounces cream cheese,
   softened
1 cup whipping cream
1 8-ounce can crushed
   pineapple

Dissolve raspberry gelatin in 1 1/3 cups boiling water in bowl. Stir in raspberries. Spoon into 8-cup mold. Chill for 20 to 30 minutes or until partially set. Dissolve lemon gelatin in 2 cups boiling water in large bowl. Stir in marshmallows. Beat cream cheese in mixer bowl until smooth. Add whipping cream gradually, beating until fluffy. Place bowl of lemon gelatin mixture in larger bowl of ice cubes. Stir until slightly thickened. Add undrained pineapple; mix well. Fold in cream cheese mixture. Spoon carefully over raspberry layer. Chill, covered, until firm. Unmold onto serving plate. Yield: 16 servings.

Approx Per Serving: Cal 214; Prot 3 g; Carbo 29 g; Fiber 1 g; T Fat 11 g; Chol 36 mg; Sod 94 mg.

*Carol J. Dorward
Washington Community High School
Washington, Illinois*

RASPBERRY-PRETZEL SALAD

3 cups crushed pretzels
1 cup melted butter
3 tablespoons sugar
8 ounces cream cheese,
  softened
1 cup confectioners' sugar
9 ounces whipped topping
2 3-ounce packages
  raspberry gelatin
2 cups boiling water
2 10-ounce packages frozen
  raspberries

Combine pretzels, butter and sugar in bowl; mix well. Spread in 9x13-inch baking dish. Bake at 350 degrees for 10 minutes. Cool to room temperature. Combine cream cheese, confectioners' sugar and whipped topping in bowl; beat until smooth. Spread over cooled pretzel layer. Dissolve gelatin in boiling water in bowl. Stir in raspberries. Chill until partially set. Spoon over cream cheese layer. Chill until set. Cut into squares. May substitute frozen strawberries and strawberry gelatin for raspberries and raspberry gelatin if preferred.
Yield: 12 servings.

Approx Per Serving: Cal 477; Prot 5 g;
Carbo 55 g; Fiber 3 g; T Fat 28 g;
Chol 62 mg; Sod 464 mg.

Karen A. Ogg, C.H.E.
Keene High School
Keene, New Hampshire

RED RASPBERRY SALAD

1 3-ounce package red
  raspberry gelatin
1 cup boiling water
1 10-ounce package frozen
  red raspberries
1 16-ounce jar applesauce

Dissolve gelatin in boiling water in bowl. Stir in raspberries and applesauce. Spoon into dish or mold. Chill overnight. Yield: 6 servings.

Approx Per Serving: Cal 134; Prot 2 g;
Carbo 33 g; Fiber 3 g; T Fat <1 g;
Chol 0 mg; Sod 47 mg.

Annette Brown
Cameron High School
Cameron, Missouri

 For a quick fruit salad dressing, use nonfat flavored yogurt in a flavor different from the fruit in the salad so another flavor is included in the salad.

RED SALAD

1 16-ounce can crushed
   pineapple
1 3-ounce package
   sugar-free raspberry gelatin
8 ounces whipped topping

Heat undrained pineapple in saucepan until bubbly. Remove from heat. Stir in gelatin until dissolved. Cool to room temperature. Fold in whipped topping. Spoon into mold or dish. Chill until set. Yield: 6 servings.

Approx Per Serving: Cal 232; Prot 2 g;
Carbo 37 g; Fiber 1 g; T Fat 10 g;
Chol 0 mg; Sod 56 mg.

Sue Lawson
Haworth School
Haworth, Oklahoma

RHUBARB SALAD

4 cups chopped rhubarb
1 cup pineapple juice
1 6-ounce package cherry
   gelatin
1 cup sugar
1 cup crushed pineapple
½ cup chopped pecans

Cook rhubarb in water to cover in saucepan until tender; drain. Bring pineapple juice to a boil in saucepan. Stir in gelatin until dissolved. Add rhubarb, sugar, pineapple and pecans; mix well. Spoon into oiled mold or shallow dish. Chill until set. May substitute applesauce for pineapple. Yield: 8 servings.

Approx Per Serving: Cal 280; Prot 3 g;
Carbo 58 g; Fiber 2 g; T Fat 5 g;
Chol 0 mg; Sod 72 mg.

Gail Brubaker
Luray High School
Luray, Virginia

 To garnish a fruit salad, peel a star fruit. Slice then dip in citrus acid like lemon or pineapple juice to keep from turning brown.

SEVEN-UP SALAD

2 cups applesauce
1   3-ounce package lime
    gelatin
1 cup 7-Up
1 cup chopped celery
1 cup chopped pecans

Heat applesauce in saucepan until bubbly. Stir in gelatin until dissolved. Add 7-Up; mix well. Chill until partially set. Add celery and pecans; mix well. Spoon into mold or dish. Chill until firm. Yield: 6 servings.

Approx Per Serving: Cal 240; Prot 3 g;
Carbo 30 g; Fiber 3 g; T Fat 14 g;
Chol 0 mg; Sod 69 mg.

Beverly Forbis
Thomas Downey High School
Modesto, California

SEVEN-UP GELATIN SALAD

2   3-ounce packages lemon
    gelatin
2 cups boiling water
1   20-ounce can crushed
    pineapple
2 cups 7-Up
3 bananas, sliced
1 cup miniature
    marshmallows
1 egg, slightly beaten
1 cup sugar
1 tablespoon flour
8 ounces whipped topping

Dissolve gelatin in boiling water in bowl. Cool to room temperature. Drain pineapple, reserving juice. Stir pineapple, 7-Up, bananas and marshmallows into gelatin. Chill until firm. Add enough water to reserved pineapple juice to measure 1 cup. Combine with egg, sugar and flour in saucepan; mix well. Cook until thickened, stirring constantly. Spread over congealed layer. Spread whipped topping over top. Chill until serving time. Yield: 15 servings.

Approx Per Serving: Cal 224; Prot 2 g;
Carbo 47 g; Fiber 1 g; T Fat 4 g;
Chol 14 mg; Sod 52 mg.

Janine Kelley
Noel Junior High School
Noel, Missouri

 All fruits and vegetables should be fresh! Fresh! Fresh!

HAWAIIAN SALAD

1 cup coconut
1 8-ounce can mandarin
   oranges
1 cup miniature
   marshmallows
1 3-ounce package pecans
8 ounces sour cream

Combine coconut, oranges, marshmallows and pecans in bowl; mix well. Fold in sour cream. Chill until serving time. Yield: 8 servings.

*Approx Per Serving: Cal 214; Prot 2 g;
Carbo 17 g; Fiber 2 g; T Fat 16 g;
Chol 13 mg; Sod 25 mg.*

Pat Phillips
Henry County High School
Paris, Tennessee

SIX-CUP SALAD

1 cup coconut
1 cup miniature
   marshmallows
1 cup pineapple chunks
1 cup mandarin oranges
1 cup blueberries
1 cup sour cream

Combine coconut, marshmallows, pineapple, oranges and blueberries in bowl; mix well. Fold in sour cream. Yield: 8 servings.

*Approx Per Serving: Cal 182; Prot 2 g;
Carbo 26 g; Fiber 3 g; T Fat 9 g;
Chol 13 mg; Sod 49 mg.*

Judith Gatewood
Forest School
Forest, Mississippi

SNOWBALL SALAD

5 large bananas
2 tablespoons lemon juice
1 16-ounce can crushed
   pineapple, drained
1/2 cup drained chopped
   maraschino cherries
1 1/2 cups chopped pecans
1 1/2 cups sugar
1 cup sour cream
24 ounces whipped topping

Mash bananas with lemon juice in 4-quart bowl. Add pineapple, cherries, pecans, sugar, sour cream and whipped topping; mix well. Spoon into 9x13-inch pan. Freeze until firm. Let stand for 30 minutes before serving. May freeze in bowl or mold and unmold to serve. Yield: 16 servings.

*Approx Per Serving: Cal 369; Prot 2 g;
Carbo 46 g; Fiber 2 g; T Fat 22 g;
Chol 6 mg; Sod 20 mg.*

Letha Wilson
Hackett High School
Hackett, Arkansas

LIGHT COTTAGE CHEESE SALAD

16 ounces low-fat cottage
  cheese
1 3-ounce package
  strawberry gelatin
1 10-ounce package frozen
  strawberries, thawed and
  drained
8 ounces whipped topping

Combine cottage cheese, gelatin, strawberries and whipped topping in bowl; mix well. Chill until serving time. May substitute other flavors of gelatin and favorite berries for strawberry gelatin and strawberries. Yield: 10 servings.

Approx Per Serving: Cal 155; Prot 7 g;
Carbo 17 g; Fiber 1 g; T Fat 7 g;
Chol 4 mg; Sod 218 mg.

Lynn M. Hughes
Riley County High School
Riley, Kansas

STRAWBERRY FLUFF

1 6-ounce package
  strawberry gelatin
1 cup boiling water
1 10-ounce package frozen
  strawberries
1 8-ounce can crushed
  pineapple
1/2 cup chopped pecans
1 10-ounce package
  miniature marshmallows
1 cup whipping cream
1 tablespoon sugar

Dissolve gelatin in boiling water in bowl. Stir in frozen strawberries, pineapple and pecans. Fold in marshmallows. Whip cream in mixer bowl until soft peaks form. Add sugar; mix well. Fold into gelatin mixture. Spoon into 9x13-inch dish. Chill until set. Cut into squares. Serve on lettuce-lined salad plates. Yield: 18 servings.

Approx Per Serving: Cal 168; Prot 2 g;
Carbo 28 g; Fiber 1 g; T Fat 6 g;
Chol 15 mg; Sod 48 mg.

Linda Honaker
Glenwood Junior High School
Princeton, West Virginia

 An easy way to peel kiwifruit is to cut off both ends. Use a soup spoon and slide the spoon under the skin and gently turn the fruit until the spoon goes all the way around. Remove spoon and fruit will slide out with a gentle push and presto—no knife marks.

STRAWBERRY-PRETZEL SALAD

2 cups crushed pretzels
1 cup melted margarine
1/4 cup sugar
8 ounces cream cheese, softened
1/2 cup sugar
1 cup whipped topping
1   6-ounce package strawberry gelatin
2 cups boiling water
2   10-ounce packages frozen strawberries, thawed and drained

Mix pretzels, margarine and 1/4 cup sugar in bowl. Spread in 9x13-inch baking dish. Bake at 400 degrees for 8 minutes. Cool to room temperature. Beat cream cheese and 1/2 cup sugar in mixer bowl until light. Blend in whipped topping. Spread over baked layer. Dissolve gelatin in boiling water in bowl. Chill until partially set. Stir in strawberries. Spread over cream cheese layer. Chill until set.
Yield: 15 servings.

Approx Per Serving: Cal 301; Prot 3 g; Carbo 31 g; Fiber 1 g; T Fat 19 g; Chol 17 mg; Sod 347 mg.

Karen Murray
Irving High School
Irving, Texas

FRESH STRAWBERRY-PRETZEL SALAD

2 cups crushed pretzels
3/4 cup melted margarine
1/4 cup sugar
8 ounces cream cheese, softened
1 cup sugar
8 ounces whipped topping
1   6-ounce package strawberry gelatin
1 cup boiling water
1 cup cold water
2 1/2 cups sliced fresh strawberries

Mix pretzels, margarine and 1/4 cup sugar in bowl. Press into 9x13-inch baking dish. Bake at 400 degrees for 8 to 10 minutes or until light brown. Cool to room temperature. Beat cream cheese with 1 cup sugar in mixer bowl until smooth. Blend in whipped topping. Spread over crust. Dissolve gelatin in 1 cup boiling water in bowl. Stir in cold water and strawberries. Spoon over cream cheese layer. Chill until set. May substitute 20 ounces frozen strawberries for fresh strawberries. Yield: 12 servings.

Approx Per Serving: Cal 408; Prot 4 g; Carbo 48 g; Fiber 1 g; T Fat 23 g; Chol 21 mg; Sod 393 mg.

Cynthia Thompson
Lonoke High School
Lonoke, Arkansas

PRETZEL SALAD

2 cups crushed pretzels
1/4 cup sugar
3/4 cup melted butter
8 ounces cream cheese,
  softened
1 cup confectioners' sugar
9 ounces whipped topping
1 6-ounce package
  strawberry gelatin
2 cups boiling water
2 10-ounce packages frozen
  strawberries

Mix pretzels, sugar and butter in bowl. Press into 9x13-inch baking dish. Bake at 400 degrees for 6 minutes. Cool to room temperature. Combine cream cheese and confectioners' sugar in mixer bowl; beat until smooth. Blend in whipped topping. Spread over crust. Dissolve gelatin in boiling water in bowl. Stir in strawberries. Chill until partially set. Spoon over cream cheese layer. Chill until set. Yield: 15 servings.

Approx Per Serving: Cal 317; Prot 3 g; Carbo 35 g; Fiber 1 g; T Fat 19 g; Chol 41 mg; Sod 285 mg.

Janice R. Weber
Eastern High School
Reedsville, Ohio

STRAWBERRY-PRETZEL CONGEALED SALAD

2 cups crushed pretzels
3/4 cup melted margarine
2 tablespoons sugar
8 ounces cream cheese,
  softened
1 cup sugar
9 ounces whipped topping
2 10-ounce packages frozen
  strawberries, thawed
2 3-ounce packages
  strawberry gelatin
2 cups boiling water

Mix pretzels, margarine and 2 tablespoons sugar in bowl. Press into 9x13-inch baking dish. Bake at 400 degrees for 10 to 12 minutes or until light brown. Cool to room temperature. Combine cream cheese, 1 cup sugar and whipped topping in mixer bowl; mix until smooth. Spread over crust. Drain strawberries, reserving juice. Dissolve gelatin in boiling water in bowl. Stir in reserved juice. Chill until partially set. Stir in strawberries. Spread over cream cheese layer. Chill until set. Yield: 12 servings.

Approx Per Serving: Cal 415; Prot 4 g; Carbo 49 g; Fiber 1 g; T Fat 24 g; Chol 21 mg; Sod 394 mg.

Vickie Bruce
Lake Hamilton Junior High School
Pearcy, Arkansas

STRAWBERRY DELIGHT

2 cups crushed pretzels
3 tablespoons sugar
¾ cup melted butter
8 ounces cream cheese,
 softened
1 cup sugar
2 cups whipped topping
1 6-ounce package
 strawberry gelatin
2 cups boiling water
1 16-ounce package frozen
 strawberries

Mix pretzels, 3 tablespoons sugar and melted butter in bowl. Press into 9x13-inch baking pan. Bake at 400 degrees for 6 minutes. Cool to room temperature. Combine cream cheese, 1 cup sugar and whipped topping in mixer bowl; beat until smooth. Spread over crust. Dissolve gelatin in boiling water in bowl. Let stand until cool. Stir in strawberries. Spoon over cream cheese layer. Chill until set. Yield: 12 servings.

Approx Per Serving: Cal 387; Prot 4 g; Carbo 47 g; Fiber 1 g; T Fat 22 g; Chol 52 mg; Sod 354 mg.

Retha Richardson
Anna High School
Anna, Texas

STRAWBERRY SALAD

2 3-ounce packages
 strawberry gelatin
1½ cups boiling water
2 10-ounce packages frozen
 strawberries
3 bananas, mashed
1 20-ounce can crushed
 pineapple, drained
1 cup chopped pecans
1 cup sour cream

Dissolve gelatin in boiling water in bowl. Add frozen strawberries. Stir until gelatin thickens. Add bananas, pineapple and pecans; mix well. Pour half the mixture into 9x13-inch dish. Chill until set. Layer sour cream and remaining gelatin over top. Chill until set.
Yield: 10 servings.

Approx Per Serving: Cal 272; Prot 4 g; Carbo 39 g; Fiber 3 g; T Fat 13 g; Chol 10 mg; Sod 69 mg.

Margaret Drvar
Monongalia County Technical Education Center
Morgantown, West Virginia

MEXICAN FRUIT SALAD

3 Delicious apples
2 avocados
1/4 cup lemon juice
1 large pineapple, peeled
  and cored
3 large oranges, peeled
1 bunch romaine lettuce,
  shredded
1 pint fresh strawberries
1/2 cup to 3/4 cup coconut
1 cup sugar
1/4 cup water
1 teaspoon grated lime rind
Juice of 2 limes

Remove core from apples; cut into wedges. Peel avocados; cut into wedges. Combine apples, avocados and lemon juice in bowl; toss to coat. Cut pineapple into cubes. Slice oranges crosswise. Place lettuce on serving plate. Arrange apples, avocados, pineapple, oranges and strawberries over lettuce. Sprinkle with coconut. Combine sugar, water, lime rind and lime juice in small bowl; mix well. Pour over salad. Yield: 12 servings.

Approx Per Serving: Cal 214; Prot 2 g;
Carbo 40 g; Fiber 7 g; T Fat 7 g;
Chol 0 mg; Sod 19 mg.

Jo Ann Sugg
Gatesville High School
Gatesville, Texas

LIGHT WALDORF GELATIN SALAD

1 6-ounce package
   sugar-free raspberry gelatin
2 cups boiling water
2 cups cold water
3/4 cup diagonally sliced
   celery
3/4 cup chopped walnuts

Dissolve gelatin in boiling water in bowl. Stir in cold water. Chill until partially set. Add celery and walnuts; mix well. Spoon into 9x13-inch dish. Chill until set. Yield: 12 servings.

Approx Per Serving: Cal 48; Prot 1 g;
Carbo 2 g; Fiber 1 g; T Fat 4 g;
Chol 0 mg; Sod 13 mg.

Marilyn Burrows
Putnam City High School
Oklahoma City, Oklahoma

 For an easy low-calorie dressing for fruit, mix 1 cup vanilla yogurt with orange juice and sweeten with 1 package of artificial sweetener.

WATERGATE SALAD

1 6-ounce package pistachio
   instant pudding mix
16 ounces whipped topping
1 20-ounce can crushed
   pineapple
1 cup drained fruit cocktail
1 cup miniature
   marshmallows
1/2 cup chopped pecans

Combine pudding mix and whipped topping in bowl; mix well. Fold in undrained pineapple, fruit cocktail, marshmallows and pecans. Chill until serving time. Yield: 12 servings.

*Approx Per Serving: Cal 270; Prot 1 g;
Carbo 40 g; Fiber 1 g; T Fat 13 g;
Chol 0 mg; Sod 110 mg.*

*M. Joanne Hughes
Shawnee Mission North High School
Shawnee Mission, Kansas*

WHITE SALAD

8 ounces cream cheese,
   softened
2 cups cottage cheese
2 cups miniature
   marshmallows
1/2 cup milk
2 cups drained crushed
   pineapple
2 cups whipped topping
1/2 cup maraschino cherries

Combine cream cheese and cottage cheese in blender container; process until smooth. Melt marshmallows with milk in saucepan, stirring to mix well; remove from heat. Combine with cheese mixture, pineapple, whipped topping and cherries in 11/2-quart bowl; mix well. Chill overnight. Yield: 10 servings.

*Approx Per Serving: Cal 253; Prot 8 g;
Carbo 25 g; Fiber 1 g; T Fat 14 g;
Chol 33 mg; Sod 257 mg.*

*Gail Brubaker
Luray High School
Luray, Virginia*

 Children like their own molded salads at mealtime or even for a snack. Use unusual-shaped utensils or containers. It's fun!

COLORFUL FRUIT SALAD

1 16-ounce can sliced
   peaches, drained
1 16-ounce can pineapple
   chunks, drained
1 11-ounce can mandarin
   oranges, drained
4 bananas, sliced
1 cup maraschino cherries
1 21-ounce can apricot pie
   filling

Combine peaches, pineapple, oranges, bananas and cherries in bowl; mix gently. Fold in pie filling. Chill, covered, until serving time. Yield: 10 servings.

Approx Per Serving: Cal 192; Prot 1 g;
Carbo 50 g; Fiber 3 g; T Fat <1 g;
Chol 0 mg; Sod 23 mg.

Jerry Stephenson
Cisco High School
Cisco, Texas

CREAMY FRUIT SALAD

1 16-ounce can pineapple
   chunks
1 4-ounce package vanilla
   instant pudding mix
1 16-ounce can apricots,
   drained, chopped
3 bananas, chopped
1 cup chopped pecans

Drain pineapple, reserving 2 tablespoons juice. Combine reserved juice with pudding mix in bowl; mix well. Add pineapple, apricots, bananas and pecans; mix well. Chill until serving time. Yield: 8 servings.

Approx Per Serving: Cal 271; Prot 2 g;
Carbo 47 g; Fiber 3 g; T Fat 10 g;
Chol 0 mg; Sod 98 mg.

Wilma Blair
Mena High School
Mena, Arkansas

FLORIDA WINTER SALAD

4 lettuce leaves
2 avocados, peeled, sliced
Sections of 2 grapefruit
3 tablespoons French salad
   dressing

Line 4 salad plates with lettuce leaves. Alternate avocado slices and grapefruit sections on prepared salad plates. Drizzle with French dressing. Yield: 4 servings.

Approx Per Serving: Cal 264; Prot 3 g;
Carbo 18 g; Fiber 12 g; T Fat 22 g;
Chol 0 mg; Sod 150 mg.

Judy B. Kiser
Marjory Stoneman Douglas High School
Parkland, Florida

FRESH FRUIT SALAD WITH ORANGE CREAM DRESSING

2 apples, unpeeled, chopped
2 bananas, chopped
1 tablespoon lemon juice
2 cups fresh strawberry
  quarters
1 fresh pineapple, peeled,
  cut into small spears
1 pound green grapes, cut
  into halves
1 cup whipping cream
1 6-ounce can frozen orange
  juice concentrate, thawed
2 tablespoons toasted
  chopped pecans

Sprinkle apples and bananas with lemon juice in bowl. Add strawberries, pineapple and grapes; toss lightly. Beat whipping cream in mixer bowl at medium speed until soft peaks form. Add orange juice concentrate gradually, beating until stiff peaks form. Spoon over fruit; sprinkle with pecans. Yield: 12 servings.

*Approx Per Serving: Cal 190; Prot 2 g;
Carbo 29 g; Fiber 3 g; T Fat 9 g;
Chol 27 mg; Sod 10 mg.*

*Hilda Harman
Smithville High School
Smithville, Mississippi*

FROZEN FRUIT SALAD

2 cups whipping cream
1/3 cup sugar
3 ounces cream cheese,
  softened
1/3 cup mayonnaise
Juice of 1 lemon
1 6-ounce can crushed
  pineapple
1 15-ounce jar maraschino
  cherries, drained
2 bananas, sliced
1 cup chopped pecans

Whip cream with sugar in mixer bowl until soft peaks form. Beat cream cheese in mixer bowl until smooth. Blend in mayonnaise and lemon juice. Fold in whipped cream, pineapple, cherries, bananas and pecans. Spoon into loaf pan. Freeze until firm. Unmold onto serving plate. Slice to serve. Yield: 12 servings.

*Approx Per Serving: Cal 363; Prot 3 g;
Carbo 27 g; Fiber 1 g; T Fat 29 g;
Chol 66 mg; Sod 71 mg.*

*Pat Chafin
Kempsville High School
Virginia Beach, Virginia*

 Reserve drained pineapple juice for soaking banana and apple slices to prevent browning before adding to recipe.

FROZEN FRUIT LOAF

1 3-ounce package
   strawberry gelatin
1 cup boiling water
1 6-ounce can frozen
   lemonade concentrate
3 cups whipped topping
1 16-ounce can sliced
   peaches, drained, chopped
1 8-ounce can pears,
   drained, chopped

Dissolve gelatin in boiling water in bowl. Add lemonade concentrate, stirring to dissolve completely. Chill until slightly thickened. Blend in whipped topping. Fold in peaches and pears. Spoon into 5x9-inch loaf pan sprayed with nonstick cooking spray. Freeze until firm. Unmold onto serving plate; slice to serve.
Yield: 12 servings.

Approx Per Serving: Cal 143; Prot 1 g; Carbo 26 g; Fiber 1 g; T Fat 5 g; Chol 0 mg; Sod 31 mg.

*Marjory L. Carpenter
Marlborough Senior High School
Marlborough, Massachusetts*

CREAMY FROZEN FRUIT SALAD

2 16-ounce cans fruit
   cocktail
1 20-ounce can sliced
   peaches
1 16-ounce can pineapple
   chunks
2 3-ounce packages lemon
   gelatin
Juice of 1 lemon
1/2 cup mayonnaise-type
   salad dressing
16 ounces cream cheese,
   softened
1 4-ounce bottle of
   maraschino cherries,
   drained
2 cups miniature
   marshmallows
1/4 teaspoon salt
8 ounces whipped topping

Drain fruit cocktail, peaches and pineapple, reserving 1 cup mixed juices. Bring reserved juices to a boil in saucepan. Combine with gelatin in bowl, stirring until gelatin is completely dissolved. Cool to room temperature. Stir in lemon juice. Combine salad dressing and cream cheese in mixer bowl; mix until smooth. Blend into gelatin. Fold in fruit cocktail, peaches, pineapple, cherries, marshmallows, salt and whipped topping. Spoon into 2 ring molds. Freeze until firm. Unmold onto serving plates. May substitute 2 cups whipped cream for whipped topping. May freeze in large pan and cut into squares to serve. Yield: 24 servings.

Approx Per Serving: Cal 222; Prot 3 g; Carbo 31 g; Fiber 1 g; T Fat 11 g; Chol 22 mg; Sod 146 mg.

*Donis L. Smith
Tylertown High School
Tylertown, Mississippi*

FROZEN PARTY SALAD

1 cup mayonnaise
8 ounces cream cheese, softened
1 20-ounce can pineapple chunks, drained
1 16-ounce can peach halves, drained
1/2 cup chopped maraschino cherries
2 tablespoons confectioners' sugar
2 cups miniature marshmallows
1 cup whipping cream, whipped

Combine mayonnaise and cream cheese in bowl; mix well. Stir in pineapple. Cut peach halves into quarters. Add peaches, maraschino cherries and confectioners' sugar to cream cheese mixture; mix well. Fold in marshmallows and whipped cream. Spoon into 5x9-inch loaf pan or individual molds. Freeze until firm. Unmold onto serving dish. May tint pink or green with food coloring before freezing if desired. Yield: 10 servings.

Approx Per Serving: Cal 428; Prot 3 g; Carbo 30 g; Fiber 1 g; T Fat 34 g; Chol 70 mg; Sod 214 mg.

Marvelyn Smith
Heritage High School
Conyers, Georgia

KAY'S FROZEN FRUIT SALAD

2 cups sour cream
16 ounces whipped topping
1 14-ounce can sweetened condensed milk
2 21-ounce cans cherry pie filling
1 16-ounce can fruit cocktail, drained
1 8-ounce can crushed pineapple, drained
1 16-ounce can sliced peaches, drained
2 16-ounce cans pitted Bing cherries, drained
1 cup chopped pecans

Combine sour cream, whipped topping and condensed milk in large bowl; mix well. Stir in pie filling. Add fruit cocktail, pineapple, peaches, Bing cherries and pecans; mix well. Spoon into loaf pans. Freeze until firm. Unmold onto serving plate; slice to serve. Yield: 40 servings.

Approx Per Serving: Cal 175; Prot 2 g; Carbo 25 g; Fiber 1 g; T Fat 8 g; Chol 8 mg; Sod 33 mg.

Kay Martin
Clarksville High School
Clarksville, Tennessee

FRUIT COMPOTE

1   21-ounce can peach pie
    filling
2   16-ounce cans pineapple,
    drained
1 pound bananas, sliced
1 pound fresh strawberries

Combine pie filling, pineapple and bananas in bowl; mix well. Add strawberries; mix well. Chill until serving time. May substitute frozen strawberries for fresh strawberries and add just before serving. Yield: 10 servings.

*Approx Per Serving: Cal 159; Prot 1 g;
Carbo 41 g; Fiber 4 g; T Fat <1 g;
Chol 0 mg; Sod 20 mg.*

Frances Ammons
Oglethorpe County High School
Lexington, Georgia

FRUIT SALAD

1   16-ounce can pineapple
    chunks
2 large apples, chopped
2 bananas, sliced
1 cup chopped pecans
1 cup strawberries
1   4-ounce package vanilla
    instant pudding mix
3 tablespoons Tang

Drain pineapple, reserving juice. Combine pineapple, apples, bananas, pecans and strawberries in bowl; mix well. Combine reserved pineapple juice, pudding mix and Tang in small bowl; mix well. Pour over fruit; toss to mix. Chill until serving time. Yield: 8 servings.

*Approx Per Serving: Cal 279; Prot 2 g;
Carbo 49 g; Fiber 4 g; T Fat 11 g;
Chol 0 mg; Sod 99 mg.*

Jean Head
Albertville High School
Albertville, Alabama

 Use bottled lime juice to thin honey for an easy, tasty fruit dressing.

TASTY FRUIT SALAD

1   20-ounce can sliced
    peaches
1   20-ounce can pears
1   16-ounce can pineapple
    tidbits
1   4-ounce package vanilla
    instant pudding mix
1   8-ounce jar maraschino
    cherries, drained
Sections of 2 oranges
2 apples, chopped
2 bananas, sliced

Drain peaches, pears and pineapple, reserving juices in large bowl. Add pudding mix; mix well. Fold in peaches, pears, pineapple, cherries, oranges, apples and bananas; mix well. Chill for 2 hours before serving. May store in refrigerator for 5 days. Yield: 12 servings.

Approx Per Serving: Cal 197; Prot 1 g;
Carbo 51 g; Fiber 3 g; T Fat <1 g;
Chol 0 mg; Sod 70 mg.

Pat Sperry
Kecoughtan High School
Hampton, Virginia

FRUIT SLUSH

Juice of 3 oranges
Juice of 3 lemons
3/4 cup sugar
1   10-ounce jar maraschino
    cherries, drained
1   20-ounce can juice-pack
    crushed pineapple
3 large bananas, sliced

Combine orange juice and lemon juice with sugar in bowl; stir until sugar is dissolved. Cut maraschino cherries into halves. Add with pineapple and bananas to juice mixture; mix well. Pour into serving dish. Freeze until firm. Let stand in refrigerator for 2 hours or until slushy before serving. May be refrozen. Yield: 8 servings.

Approx Per Serving: Cal 209; Prot 1 g;
Carbo 54 g; Fiber 2 g; T Fat <1 g;
Chol 0 mg; Sod 3 mg.

Johnanna Hunt
Polk County High School
Benton, Tennessee

 Freeze red or white grapes for a delicious cool summer treat.

HAWAIIAN FRUIT COCKTAIL

1 cup pineapple chunks
1 cup orange sections
3/4 cup melon balls
2 bananas, sliced
1 cup whole fresh
    strawberries
1 cup chopped apples
1/4 cup honey
1/4 cup lemon juice

Combine pineapple, orange, melon, bananas, strawberries and apples in serving bowl. Mix honey and lemon juice in bowl. Pour over fruit. Chill until serving time. Garnish with mint leaves. Yield: 6 servings.

*Approx Per Serving: Cal 153; Prot 1 g;
Carbo 40 g; Fiber 3 g; T Fat <1 g;
Chol 0 mg; Sod 9 mg.*

*Mary O. Giles
Poquoson Middle School
Poquoson, Virginia*

MAKE-AHEAD FRUIT SALAD

2   16-ounce cans chunky
    fruit
2   20-ounce cans pineapple
    chunks
1   11-ounce can mandarin
    oranges
1/2 cup orange juice
2   4-ounce packages vanilla
    pudding mix
3 or 4 bananas, sliced

Drain chunky fruit, pineapple and mandarin oranges, reserving 2 1/2 cups mixed fruit juices. Combine reserved mixed fruit juices, orange juice and pudding mix in saucepan. Cook until thickened. Cool. Combine chunky fruit, pineapple, mandarin oranges and bananas in large bowl; mix well. Stir in cooled pudding. Chill for 8 hours to overnight. May add strawberries, grapes, blueberries or other fruit for color. Yield: 12 servings.

*Approx Per Serving: Cal 254; Prot 1 g;
Carbo 65 g; Fiber 3 g; T Fat <1 g;
Chol 0 mg; Sod 134 mg.*

*Mildred Polovich
Gillespie High School
Gillespie, Illinois*

 Use chilled salad plates or dessert cups for gelatin salads in warm weather.

MAMA'S FRUIT SALAD

1/2 4-ounce jar maraschino
    cherries
3 apples, chopped
3 bananas, sliced
1 16-ounce can fruit
    cocktail, drained
1 20-ounce can crushed
    pineapple, drained
Sections of 4 oranges
Cooked Whipped Cream
    Dressing (page 116)

Cut maraschino cherries into halves. Combine cherries, apples, bananas, fruit cocktail, pineapple and oranges in large bowl; mix well. Add Cooked Whipped Cream Dressing; mix well. Chill until serving time. Yield: 10 servings.

Approx Per Serving: Cal 278; Prot 3 g;
Carbo 58 g; Fiber 4 g; T Fat 6 g;
Chol 39 mg; Sod 48 mg.

Doris Stults
Collinwood High School
Collinwood, Tennessee

MOTHER-IN-LAW'S FRUIT SALAD

3 bananas, sliced
3 apples, chopped
Sections from 3 oranges
1 cup cherries
1 cup grape halves
1 cup pineapple tidbits
Cooked Fruit Dressing
    (page 116)
1 pint whipping cream,
    whipped

Combine bananas, apples, oranges, cherries, grapes and pineapple in large bowl; mix well. Fold in Cooked Fruit Dressing and whipped cream. Chill until serving time. Yield: 8 servings.

Approx Per Serving: Cal 483; Prot 4 g;
Carbo 55 g; Fiber 4 g; T Fat 30 g;
Chol 150 mg; Sod 75 mg.

Shirley Davis
Rockwood High School
Rockwood, Tennessee

MY SOUR CREAM FRUIT SALAD

1 cup drained pineapple
    chunks
1 cup drained orange sections
1 cup flaked coconut
1 cup miniature
    marshmallows
1/2 cup maraschino cherries
1 cup sour cream

Combine pineapple, orange, coconut, marshmallows and maraschino cherries in bowl; mix well. Fold in sour cream. Yield: 4 servings.

Approx Per Serving: Cal 322; Prot 3 g;
Carbo 40 g; Fiber 4 g; T Fat 18 g;
Chol 26 mg; Sod 51 mg.

Diane Howell
FDJ Vocational Center
York, South Carolina

OUR FAMILY FRUIT SALAD

1   8-ounce can pineapple
    chunks
1 egg, beaten
1/2 cup sugar
1 tablespoon (heaping) flour
1 tablespoon lemon juice
1   20-ounce can fruit
    cocktail, drained
2 bananas, sliced
1/2 cup miniature
    marshmallows
1/2 cup chopped walnuts

Drain pineapple, reserving 3/4 cup to 1 cup juice. Combine reserved juice, egg, sugar, flour and lemon juice in saucepan; mix well. Cook over medium heat until slightly thickened, stirring constantly. Cool. Combine pineapple with remaining ingredients in bowl. Stir in cooled dressing. Chill, covered, until serving time. Yield: 8 servings.

Approx Per Serving: Cal 211; Prot 3 g;
Carbo 41 g; Fiber 2 g; T Fat 6 g;
Chol 27 mg; Sod 18 mg.

Ruth Terzynski
SPASH
Stevens Point, Wisconsin

QUICK FRUIT YUM

1   21-ounce can peach pie
    filling
1   11-ounce can mandarin
    oranges, drained
1   15-ounce can pineapple
    tidbits, drained
10 fresh strawberries, sliced

Combine all ingredients in bowl; mix well. Chill until serving time. Yield: 6 servings.

Approx Per Serving: Cal 164; Prot 1 g;
Carbo 43 g; Fiber 3 g; T Fat <1 g;
Chol 0 mg; Sod 34 mg.

Sabrina Bennett
Madison County High School
Danielsville, Georgia

YUMMY FRUIT SALAD

1 cup mandarin oranges,
    drained
1 cup pineapple chunks,
    drained
1 cup coconut
1 cup marshmallows
1 cup sour cream

Combine mandarin oranges, pineapple, coconut and marshmallows in bowl; mix well. Stir in sour cream. Chill until serving time. Yield: 6 servings.

Approx Per Serving: Cal 217; Prot 2 g;
Carbo 27 g; Fiber 3 g; T Fat 12 g;
Chol 17 mg; Sod 34 mg.

Grace C. Gibson
Kemper County High School
DeKalb, Mississippi

Salads Salads Salads Salads Salads
Salads Salads Salads Salads Salads
Salads Salads Salads Salads Salads
Salads Salads Salads Salads Salads

PASTAS

PASTA SALAD

16 ounces small pasta shells, cooked
1/2 cup ranch salad dressing
1 small red onion, chopped
1 small green bell pepper, chopped
1 cup Parmesan cheese
1 tomato, chopped
3 cups chopped cooked chicken

Combine pasta and dressing in bowl; mix well. Add remaining ingredients; toss to mix. Serve on lettuce-lined salad plates. Yield: 12 servings.

Approx Per Serving: Cal 280; Prot 18 g; Carbo 31 g; Fiber 2 g; T Fat 9 g; Chol 40 mg; Sod 201 mg.

Jan Arthur
Union Public School
Union, Mississippi

MAIN DISH PASTA SALAD

4 ounces corkscrew noodles, cooked
2 cups cooked broccoli flowerets
8 ounces Cheddar cheese, shredded
1 cup chopped ham
1 teaspoon dillweed
1 cup light mayonnaise
Salt to taste

Combine all ingredients in bowl; mix well. Chill for 4 hours or longer. Yield: 6 servings.

Approx Per Serving: Cal 360; Prot 19 g; Carbo 22 g; Fiber 2 g; T Fat 22 g; Chol 63 mg; Sod 753 mg.

Patricia Williamson
Chattanooga Central High School
Harrison, Tennessee

ENGLISH PEA AND PASTA SALAD

1 cup elbow macaroni, cooked
1   16-ounce can English peas, drained
1   2-ounce jar chopped pimento, drained
4 ounces Cheddar cheese, cubed
1 small onion, chopped
1/2 to 1 cup mayonnaise-type salad dressing

Combine macaroni, peas, pimento, cheese and onion in bowl; mix well. Add salad dressing; toss to mix. Chill for 10 to 15 minutes before serving. Yield: 6 servings.

Approx Per Serving: Cal 345; Prot 10 g; Carbo 33 g; Fiber 4 g; T Fat 20 g; Chol 30 mg; Sod 604 mg.

Jodie Ellzey
L. V. Berkner High School
Richardson, Texas

FROG EYE SALAD

1/2 cup sugar
1/4 teaspoon salt
1 tablespoon flour
2 egg yolks, beaten
1 15-ounce can pineapple
   tidbits
1 15-ounce can crushed
   pineapple
1 cup uncooked acini-de-pepe
3 cups miniature
   marshmallows
1 11-ounce can mandarin
   oranges, drained
8 ounces whipped topping
1 cup coconut
1 4-ounce jar maraschino
   cherries, drained, chopped

Combine sugar, salt, flour and eggs in medium saucepan. Drain pineapple, reserving 1 cup juice. Add reserved juice to saucepan; mix well. Cook over low heat until thickened, stirring constantly. Cool. Cook pasta using package directions until just tender; drain. Rinse quickly with cold water; drain. Combine pasta with cooled dressing in bowl; mix well. Chill overnight. Pasta will absorb liquid. Add pineapple, marshmallows, mandarin oranges, whipped topping, coconut and maraschino cherries; mix well. Yield: 20 servings.

Approx Per Serving: Cal 152; Prot 2 g;
Carbo 31 g; Fiber 1 g; T Fat 3 g;
Chol 22 mg; Sod 45 mg.

Judy Adler
Snyder High School
Snyder, Oklahoma

ITALIAN SAUSAGE AND PASTA SALAD

8 ounces sweet or hot Italian
   sausage
8 ounces spiral pasta
1/2 medium green bell pepper
1/2 medium red bell pepper
1 medium onion
1 15-ounce can kidney
   beans, drained
1/2 cup red wine vinegar and
   oil salad dressing
2 tablespoons chopped
   parsley
1/2 teaspoon soy sauce
1/8 teaspoon hot pepper sauce
1 clove of garlic, minced
1/2 teaspoon salt
Freshly ground pepper to
   taste

Cook sausage in water to cover for 3 minutes; drain. Cut into 1/2-inch slices. Brown in skillet, stirring frequently; drain. Cook pasta using package directions; drain. Cut green pepper, red pepper and onion into thin slices. Combine with sausage, pasta and kidney beans in large bowl; toss to mix. Mix salad dressing, parsley, soy sauce, hot pepper sauce, garlic and salt in small bowl. Pour over salad. Add pepper; toss to mix. Chill for several hours before serving. Yield: 4 servings.

Approx Per Serving: Cal 589; Prot 23 g;
Carbo 75 g; Fiber 13 g; T Fat 26 g;
Chol 21 mg; Sod 705 mg.

Melinda Hamilton
Cass District Junior High School
Osage, West Virginia

ITALIAN PASTA AND SALMON SALAD

2 cups cooked medium shell
  macaroni
4 radishes, sliced
1/2 medium green bell
  pepper, chopped
2 green onions, thinly sliced
1/4 cup shredded carrot
1/3 cup oil
3 tablespoons white wine
  vinegar
1 clove of garlic, minced
1/2 teaspoon basil
1/4 teaspoon dry mustard
1 cup cherry tomato halves
2 6-ounce cans pink
  salmon, drained

Combine macaroni, radishes, green pepper, green onions and carrot in bowl; mix well. Combine oil, vinegar, garlic, basil and mustard in small bowl; mix well. Add to macaroni mixture; toss to mix. Chill for 2 hours to overnight. Add tomatoes and salmon just before serving; toss gently. Yield: 6 servings.

Approx Per Serving: Cal 164; Prot 14 g;
Carbo 16 g; Fiber 2 g; T Fat 5 g;
Chol 25 mg; Sod 310 mg.

Melody Walker
L. V. Berkner High School
Richardson, Texas

ITALIAN VEGETABLE TOSS

1 1/2 cups shell macaroni
2 cups broccoli flowerets
1 cup cauliflowerets
1 cup sliced mushrooms
1 6-ounce can artichoke
  hearts
1/2 cup chopped green onions
1 cup sliced pitted black
  olives
2/3 cup Italian salad dressing
1 medium avocado
1 medium tomato

Cook macaroni using package directions; drain. Cool. Combine cooled macaroni, broccoli, cauliflower and mushrooms in bowl. Drain artichoke hearts; rinse and chop. Add artichoke hearts, green onions and olives to macaroni; mix well. Add salad dressing; toss to mix. Chill, covered, for several hours. Peel and slice avocado. Seed and chop tomato. Add avocado and tomato to salad just before serving; toss to mix. Yield: 12 servings.

Approx Per Serving: Cal 162; Prot 3 g;
Carbo 12 g; Fiber 4 g; T Fat 15 g;
Chol 0 mg; Sod 224 mg.

Jean Nixon
Barton Junior High School
El Dorado, Arkansas

STIR-FRY VEGETABLE-STYLE LINGUINE

8 ounces linguine
2 tablespoons oil
1 shallot, finely chopped
2 cloves of garlic, minced
2 tablespoons sesame seed
Flowerets of 1/2 bunch
    broccoli
2 carrots, thinly sliced
1 cup chicken broth
1/2 cup Parmesan cheese
Pepper to taste

Cook linguine using package directions; drain. Preheat wok to 250 degrees. Add oil, shallot, garlic, sesame seed, broccoli and carrots. Stir-fry for 2 minutes or until vegetables are tender-crisp. Add pasta, chicken broth, cheese and pepper. Cook for 2 minutes longer or until cheese is melted, stirring constantly. Yield: 4 servings.

Approx Per Serving: Cal 411; Prot 17 g;
Carbo 57 g; Fiber 6 g; T Fat 14 g;
Chol 8 mg; Sod 414 mg.

Barbara Teman
Atlantic High School
Delray Beach, Florida

CHEDDAR MACARONI SALAD

3 cups medium shell
    macaroni
2 cups Cheddar cheese cubes
1 cup chopped celery
1/2 cup chopped green bell
    pepper
1/2 cup chopped onion
1 cup sour cream
1 cup mayonnaise-type salad
    dressing
1/4 cup milk
1/2 cup sweet pickle relish
4 teaspoons vinegar
1 1/2 teaspoons prepared
    mustard
3/4 teaspoon salt

Cook macaroni using package directions; drain. Cool to room temperature. Combine macaroni, cheese, celery, green pepper and onion in bowl; mix well. Combine sour cream, salad dressing and milk in small bowl; mix well. Stir in relish, vinegar, mustard and salt. Add to macaroni mixture; toss to mix. Salad will appear very moist. Chill, covered, for several hours before serving. Serve in lettuce-lined salad bowl. Garnish with green pepper rings. Yield: 12 servings.

Approx Per Serving: Cal 268; Prot 8 g;
Carbo 21 g; Fiber 1 g; T Fat 17 g;
Chol 34 mg; Sod 491 mg.

Donna McKethan
Bosqueville High School
Waco, Texas

 To seed a tomato, cut in half, squeeze, and shake over disposal.

MACARONI SALAD

1/2 cup sugar
1 1/2 teaspoons salt
1 teaspoon pepper
1 cup mayonnaise-type salad
  dressing
8 ounces shell macaroni,
  cooked
1 cup chopped celery
1 tomato, chopped
1 cucumber, peeled, chopped
1 green bell pepper, chopped
1 onion, chopped

Combine sugar, salt, pepper and salad dressing in small bowl; mix well. Combine macaroni, celery, tomato, cucumber, green pepper and onion in large bowl; mix well. Add dressing; toss to mix. Chill until serving time. Yield: 6 servings.

Approx Per Serving: Cal 383; Prot 6 g; Carbo 60 g; Fiber 3 g; T Fat 14 g; Chol 10 mg; Sod 834 mg.

Marla Prusa
Clarkson Public High School
Clarkson, Nebraska

TUNA-MACARONI SALAD

8 ounces small shell
  macaroni, cooked
1 cup mayonnaise-type salad
  dressing
1 tablespoon chopped onion
1 1/2 teaspoons salt
1/4 teaspoon pepper
1 6-ounce can water-pack
  tuna, drained
1/4 cup chopped green bell
  pepper

Combine macaroni, salad dressing and onion in bowl; mix well. Cool. Add salt, pepper, tuna and green pepper; mix well. Chill until serving time. Yield: 6 servings.

Approx Per Serving: Cal 331; Prot 14 g; Carbo 38 g; Fiber 2 g; T Fat 14 g; Chol 26 mg; Sod 913 mg.

Kathryn T. Stewart
Franklin County High School
Winchester, Tennessee

ROTINI SALAD

16 ounces rotini, cooked
2 green bell peppers,
  chopped
2 tomatoes, chopped
1/2 onion, chopped
Sweet Sesame Dressing
  (page 120)

Chill rotini in refrigerator. Combine with vegetables and Sweet Sesame Dressing in bowl; toss to mix. Chill for 2 hours. Yield: 25 servings.

Approx Per Serving: Cal 174; Prot 2 g; Carbo 32 g; Fiber 1 g; T Fat 5 g; Chol 0 mg; Sod 138 mg.

Jean Ann Sadler
Southside High School
Fort Smith, Arkansas

CHEF'S PASTA SALAD

8 ounces curly macaroni
1 4-ounce can chopped
   mushrooms
1 cup frozen peas
1 cup finely chopped
   tomatoes
1 cup chopped ham
1/2 cup finely chopped green
   onions
1/2 cup chopped mango
1 cup Cheddar cheese cubes
1¹/2 cups ranch salad dressing
1/2 cup Italian salad dressing

Cook macaroni using package directions; drain. Cool. Combine macaroni, mushrooms, peas, tomatoes, ham, green onions, mango and cheese in bowl; mix well. Add ranch dressing and Italian dressing; mix well. Chill for 2 to 4 hours. Stir well just before serving. May omit mushrooms and tomatoes and store in refrigerator for several days. May substitute chicken for ham. Yield: 10 servings.

*Approx Per Serving: Cal 359; Prot 12 g;
Carbo 25 g; Fiber 3 g; T Fat 26 g;
Chol 34 mg; Sod 537 mg.*

*Barbara Grimes
Northeast High School
Arma, Kansas*

REGINA'S QUICK PASTA SALAD

12 ounces colored spiral
   noodles
8 ounces lean ham
8 ounces pepperoni
1 16-ounce jar marinated
   artichokes, drained
1 16-ounce can whole black
   olives
1 cup shredded mozzarella
   cheese
1 10-ounce bottle of zesty
   Italian salad dressing

Cook noodles using package directions; drain. Cool. Cut ham and pepperoni into julienne strips. Cut artichokes and olives into quarters. Combine noodles, ham, pepperoni, artichokes, olives and cheese in bowl; mix well. Add salad dressing; toss to mix. Marinate, covered, overnight in refrigerator. Yield: 8 servings.

*Approx Per Serving: Cal 697; Prot 23 g;
Carbo 43 g; Fiber 8 g; T Fat 56 g;
Chol 36 mg; Sod 1910 mg.*

*Regina Hall
Lancaster High School
Lancaster, Texas*

 If a pasta or potato salad prepared with mayonnaise appears too liquidy, place a fresh slice of white bread on top of the salad to absorb the excess liquid.

MEXICAN PASTA SALAD

1½ cups cooked small shell
  macaroni
1 medium tomato, chopped
¼ cup chopped onion
1 green bell pepper, chopped
½ clove of garlic, minced
1 medium green chili pepper,
  seeded, chopped
1 tablespoon olive oil
1½ teaspoons red wine
  vinegar
1½ teaspoons lime juice
¼ teaspoon salt
⅛ teaspoon oregano
⅛ teaspoon pepper

Combine macaroni, tomato, onion, green pepper and garlic in glass bowl; mix well. Combine chili pepper, olive oil, vinegar, lime juice, salt, oregano and pepper in small bowl; mix well. Add to salad; toss to mix. Chill, covered, until serving time. Toss to mix just before serving. Yield: 2 servings.

Approx Per Serving: Cal 241; Prot 7 g; Carbo 38 g; Fiber 4 g; T Fat 8 g; Chol 0 mg; Sod 277 mg.

Debbie Mock
Central Heights High School
Richmond, Kansas

PASTA AND BEAN SALAD

8 ounces rotini
1 pound Kielbasa smoked
  sausage
1 tablespoon oil
1   8-ounce can red kidney
  beans
1 small onion, chopped
1 green bell pepper, finely
  chopped
1   15-ounce can 3-bean salad
2½ tablespoons cider vinegar
½ teaspoon salt
⅛ teaspoon pepper
1 tomato, chopped
1 cucumber, chopped
6 tablespoons mayonnaise
3½ tablespoons Dijon
  mustard

Cook pasta using package directions; drain. Peel sausage; cut into ¼-inch slices. Sauté sausage in oil in skillet; drain. Rinse kidney beans; drain. Combine sausage, kidney beans, onion, green pepper and 3-bean salad in bowl; mix well. Sprinkle vinegar, salt and pepper over pasta in bowl; toss to mix. Add pasta, tomato and cucumber to bean mixture; mix well. Add mixture of mayonnaise and mustard; toss to mix. Chill for several hours before serving. Yield: 4 servings.

Approx Per Serving: Cal 687; Prot 22 g; Carbo 70 g; Fiber 12 g; T Fat 36 g; Chol 47 mg; Sod 1666 mg.

Brenda M. Deitz
West Caldwell High School
Lenoir, North Carolina

PASTA SALAD WITH HAM

12 ounces tri-colored spiral
  pasta
1 tablespoon olive oil
¼ cup (or more) Italian salad
  dressing
4 to 8 ounces fresh
  mushrooms
2 carrots, thinly sliced
2 stalks celery, sliced
2 cups broccoli flowerets
2 green onions, thinly sliced
¼ teaspoon garlic powder
1 tablespoon olive oil
Juice of ½ lemon
¾ teaspoon basil
8 ounces Monterey Jack
  cheese, cut into cubes
8 ounces ham, cut into cubes

Cook pasta using package directions with 1 tablespoon olive oil; drain. Rinse with cold water; drain. Combine pasta and salad dressing in large bowl; toss to mix. Cut mushrooms into quarters. Add mushrooms, carrots, celery, broccoli, green onions, garlic powder, 1 tablespoon olive oil, lemon juice and basil to pasta; mix well. Chill until serving time. Add cheese and ham just before serving. Yield: 12 servings.

Approx Per Serving: Cal 263; Prot 14 g;
Carbo 25 g; Fiber 3 g; T Fat 12 g;
Chol 28 mg; Sod 391 mg.

Susan Baker
MacArthur High School
Houston, Texas

PASTA SALAD WITH SHRIMP

½ cup sour cream
2 tablespoons instant beef
  bouillon
1½ cups mayonnaise
16 ounces pasta
2 green bell peppers
1 medium onion
3 or 4 stalks celery
2 4-ounce cans chopped
  black olives
1 pound peeled, cooked
  shrimp

Combine sour cream, instant bouillon and mayonnaise in small bowl; mix well. Let stand until bouillon is dissolved; mix well. Cook pasta using package directions; drain. Rinse with cold water; drain. Chop green peppers, onion and celery. Combine chopped vegetables, pasta, olives and shrimp in large bowl. Add dressing; toss to mix. Chill until serving time. May add chopped tomatoes if desired. Yield: 8 servings.

Approx Per Serving: Cal 663; Prot 21 g;
Carbo 49 g; Fiber 5 g; T Fat 44 g;
Chol 142 mg; Sod 1261 mg.

Barbara Benson
Shawnee Mission South High School
Overland Park, Kansas

PASTA AND VEGETABLE MEDLEY

6 ounces pasta
3 tablespoons butter
2 cups sliced carrots
2 cups broccoli flowerets
2 small zucchini, sliced
5 green onions, sliced
1/2 green bell pepper,
   chopped
1/2 red bell pepper, chopped
1 teaspoon basil
1 cup sour cream
1/2 cup buttermilk
1/2 teaspoon seasoned salt
3 tablespoons Dijon mustard
2/3 cup Parmesan cheese

Cook pasta using package directions; drain. Rinse in hot water; drain. Keep warm. Melt butter in wok. Stir-fry carrots for 1 minute. Add broccoli, zucchini, green onions, green pepper, red pepper and basil. Stir-fry for 2 to 3 minutes or until tender-crisp. Remove to warm bowl. Stir in pasta. Mix sour cream, buttermilk, seasoned salt and mustard in saucepan. Cook over medium heat until warm. Stir in cheese. Cook until cheese is melted, stirring constantly. Pour over vegetables; toss to mix. Yield: 6 servings.

Approx Per Serving: Cal 331; Prot 12 g;
Carbo 33 g; Fiber 5 g; T Fat 18 g;
Chol 40 mg; Sod 555 mg.

Susan W. Bigelow
Westover Junior High School
Morgantown, West Virginia

VEGETABLE AND PASTA SALAD

16 ounces curly macaroni
1½ cups sugar
1 cup white vinegar
1 cup oil
1½ cups chopped green
   onions
1 cup chopped carrots
1 cup finely chopped green
   bell peppers
1 cup sliced radishes
1 cup sliced celery
1 medium head lettuce

Cook macaroni using package directions; drain. Heat sugar, vinegar and oil in saucepan until sugar dissolves, stirring constantly. Pour over macaroni in bowl; mix well. Marinate in refrigerator overnight. Add green onions, carrots, green peppers, radishes and celery to macaroni mixture; toss to mix. Chill until serving time. Tear lettuce into bite-sized pieces. Add to salad just before serving; toss to mix.
Yield: 20 servings.

Approx Per Serving: Cal 249; Prot 3 g;
Carbo 35 g; Fiber 2 g; T Fat 11 g;
Chol 0 mg; Sod 12 mg.

Nancy M. Riley
Waterford High School
Waterford, Ohio

ITALIAN SPAGHETTI SALAD

16 ounces spaghetti
3 small zucchini
3 green bell peppers
3 medium red onions
1   8-ounce bottle of
    Wishbone Italian salad
    dressing
1/2 bottle of Salad Supreme
    seasoning
3 tomatoes, chopped

Break spaghetti into quarters. Cook spaghetti using package directions; drain. Peel zucchini; cut into cubes. Chop green peppers and onions fine. Combine spaghetti, zucchini, green peppers, onions, salad dressing and seasoning in bowl; mix well. Chill overnight. Add tomatoes just before serving; toss to mix. Yield: 12 servings.

Approx Per Serving: Cal 258; Prot 6 g;
Carbo 37 g; Fiber 3 g; T Fat 12 g;
Chol 0 mg; Sod 98 mg.
Nutritional analysis does not include
Salad Supreme seasoning.

Nancy Goodson
Roxana High School
Roxana, Illinois

SPAGHETTI SALAD

16 ounces spaghetti
1 green bell pepper, chopped
1 onion, chopped
1 cucumber, chopped
1 tomato, chopped
1 carrot, grated
1 bottle of Salad Supreme
    seasoning
1   12-ounce bottle of light
    Italian salad dressing

Break spaghetti into quarters. Cook spaghetti using package directions; drain. Cool. Combine spaghetti, green pepper, onion, cucumber, tomato, carrot, seasoning and salad dressing in bowl. Marinate in refrigerator for 6 hours to overnight. Serve at room temperature. Yield: 12 servings.

Approx Per Serving: Cal 169; Prot 5 g;
Carbo 33 g; Fiber 3 g; T Fat 2 g;
Chol 2 mg; Sod 228 mg.
Nutritional analysis does not include
Salad Supreme seasoning.

Sharon Rhudy
Tazewell High School
Tazewell, Virginia

LEMON SPAGHETTI SALAD

12 ounces spaghetti
1 tablespoon MSG
2 tablespoons seasoned salt
3 tablespoons lemon juice
1/4 cup oil
1 cup chopped celery
1/2 cup chopped onion
1/2 cup chopped green bell
　pepper
1/2 cup sliced olives
1/2 cup chopped pimentos
1 1/2 cups mayonnaise

Cook spaghetti using package directions; drain. Add MSG, seasoned salt, lemon juice and oil; toss to mix. Marinate in dressing in refrigerator for 2 days. Add celery, onion, green pepper, olives, pimentos and mayonnaise; mix well. Chill until serving time. May omit MSG. Yield: 12 servings.

Approx Per Serving: Cal 361; Prot 4 g; Carbo 24 g; Fiber 2 g; T Fat 28 g; Chol 16 mg; Sod 2530 mg.

Connie Morrill
Chadwick Junior High School
Chadwick, Missouri

ORIENTAL TORTELINI SALAD

1 16-ounce package frozen
　tortelini
1 16-ounce package frozen
　oriental vegetables
4 teaspoons prepared
　mustard
1/4 cup wine vinegar
1/3 cup olive oil
1/2 teaspoon garlic powder
2 tablespoons lemon juice
1/2 teaspoon oregano
3/4 teaspoon salt
1/8 teaspoon pepper
1 teaspoon basil
1/2 cup Parmesan cheese

Cook tortelini using package directions. Place oriental vegetables in colander. Pour cooked tortelini over vegetables. Combine mustard, vinegar, olive oil, garlic powder, lemon juice, oregano, salt, pepper and basil in large bowl; mix well. Add tortelini and vegetables; toss to coat. Sprinkle with cheese. Serve warm or chill in refrigerator for 2 hours before serving. Yield: 6 servings.

Approx Per Serving: Cal 464; Prot 15 g; Carbo 68 g; Fiber 6 g; T Fat 15 g; Chol 5 mg; Sod 464 mg.

Teresa R. Nash Sitek, C.H.E. and Maria F. Nash
Pembroke Junior/Senior High School
Corfu, New York

Salads Salads Salads Salads Salads
Salads Salads Salads Salads Salads
Salads Salads Salads Salads Salads
Salads Salads Salads Salads Salads

VEGETABLES

ASPARAGUS TOSS

1 medium onion, sliced
3 medium tomatoes, cut into
  wedges
1 small green bell pepper,
  cut into strips
1   20-ounce can asparagus
  spears, chilled, drained
Garlic Vinaigrette (page 122)
3 hard-boiled eggs, cut into
  wedges

Separate sliced onion into rings. Combine with tomatoes and green pepper in salad bowl; mix gently. Add asparagus; toss to mix. Shake Garlic Vinaigrette to mix well. Add to salad; toss gently. Serve on lettuce-lined salad plates. Top with eggs. Yield: 6 servings.

*Approx Per Serving: Cal 163; Prot 6 g;
Carbo 8 g; Fiber 3 g; T Fat 13 g;
Chol 106 mg; Sod 419 mg.*

*Virginia Dare Garber
Grundy Senior High School
Grundy, Virginia*

GREEN BEAN SALAD

2   16-ounce cans green
  beans, drained
1/4 cup thinly sliced onion
1 tablespoon vinegar
1 tablespoon oil
1/2 teaspoon salt
1/2 cup sour cream
1/4 cup mayonnaise
1/2 teaspoon lemon juice
2 tablespoons horseradish
1/8 teaspoon dry mustard
Minced garlic to taste

Combine beans, onion, vinegar, oil and salt in bowl; toss gently. Marinate in refrigerator for 1 hour. Drain well. Combine sour cream, mayonnaise, lemon juice, horseradish and dry mustard in small bowl; mix well. Add to salad; mix gently. Serve on lettuce-lined salad plates. Sprinkle with garlic. Garnish with onion croutons. Yield: 6 servings.

*Approx Per Serving: Cal 161; Prot 3 g;
Carbo 9 g; Fiber 2 g; T Fat 14 g;
Chol 14 mg; Sod 625 mg.
Nutritional information includes
entire amount of marinade.*

*Karen Meyer
Shawnee Mission North High School
Shawnee Mission, Kansas*

 Layer asparagus spears and peas in dish. Top with Italian dressing prepared with wine instead of vinegar. Garnish with pimento, lemon pepper and/or Parmesan cheese.

GREEN BEAN AND CORN SALAD

1   16-ounce can French-style
    green beans, drained
1   16-ounce can Shoe Peg
    corn, drained
1 medium onion, sliced into
    rings
1 medium green bell pepper,
    sliced into rings
1 cup chopped celery
1/2 cup oil
1/2 cup vinegar
1/2 cup sugar

Combine green beans and corn in 2-quart bowl.
Add onion, green pepper and celery; mix well.
Heat oil, vinegar and sugar in saucepan, stirring
until sugar is dissolved. Pour over vegetables;
mix gently. Chill overnight. Yield: 8 servings.

*Approx Per Serving: Cal 239; Prot 3 g;
Carbo 29 g; Fiber 2 g; T Fat 14 g;
Chol 0 mg; Sod 288 mg.*

*Betty Evans
Blue Ridge High School
Blue Ridge, Texas*

SCANDINAVIAN BEAN SALAD

1   20-ounce can French-style
    green beans, drained
1   20-ounce can green peas,
    drained
1 small green bell pepper,
    chopped
4 stalks celery, coarsely
    chopped
1 small onion, thinly sliced
    into rings
1   2-ounce jar chopped
    pimento
3/4 cup sugar
1 cup vinegar
1/2 cup oil
Paprika to taste

Layer beans, peas, green pepper, celery, onion
and pimento in bowl. Combine sugar, vinegar,
oil and paprika in saucepan. Heat over medium
heat until sugar is dissolved, stirring constantly.
Cool to room temperature. Pour over vegetables. Chill for 24 hours to 4 days.
Yield: 10 servings.

*Approx Per Serving: Cal 217; Prot 4 g;
Carbo 28 g; Fiber 4 g; T Fat 11 g;
Chol 0 mg; Sod 282 mg.*

*Lucille H. Wiggins
I.C. Norcom High School
Portsmouth, Virginia*

 *Different vinegars can be used for variety in salad dressings. Try
tarragon, red wine or white wine vinegars. Garlic, salt and freshly ground pepper are basic spices—others might include savory,
basil, tarragon, oregano, chives, parsley, chervil and marjoram.*

BROCCOLI AND CAULIFLOWER SALAD

1 bunch broccoli, chopped
Flowerets of 1 head cauliflower
1 ounce chopped pimento
1   8-ounce can sliced water
   chestnuts, drained
1   16-ounce can kidney
   beans, drained
1 cup shredded sharp
   Cheddar cheese
1/2 cup crumbled crisp-fried
   bacon
1   8-ounce bottle of Italian
   salad dressing

Combine broccoli, cauliflower, pimento, water chestnuts and beans in bowl; mix well. Add cheese, bacon and salad dressing; toss lightly. Chill until serving time. Yield: 8 servings.

Approx Per Serving: Cal 319; Prot 12 g;
Carbo 25 g; Fiber 8 g; T Fat 24 g;
Chol 18 mg; Sod 300 mg.

Wendy Bokus
Schuylerville, Junior-Senior High School
Schuylerville, New York

BROCCOLI AND CHEDDAR SALAD

Chopped flowerets of 1 head
   broccoli
1/2 onion, finely chopped
2 cups shredded Cheddar
   cheese
8 ounces bacon, crisp-fried,
   crumbled
1/2 cup mayonnaise
2 tablespoons vinegar
1/2 cup sugar

Combine broccoli, onion, cheese and bacon in salad bowl; mix well. Mix mayonnaise, vinegar and sugar in small bowl. Add to salad; mix well. Chill, covered, for several hours. Yield: 8 servings.

Approx Per Serving: Cal 325; Prot 11 g;
Carbo 17 g; Fiber 2 g; T Fat 25 g;
Chol 45 mg; Sod 402 mg.

Gail Helms
Enterprise High School
Enterprise, Alabama

BROCCOLI AND PECAN SALAD

Flowerets of 1 head broccoli
1 medium red onion, chopped
1/2 cup chopped celery
1 cup raisins
10 slices crisp-fried bacon,
   crumbled
1 cup chopped pecans
1 cup mayonnaise
1/4 cup vinegar
3 tablespoons sugar

Combine first 6 ingredients in bowl; mix well. Stir in mixture of mayonnaise, vinegar and sugar. Chill for 6 hours or longer. Yield: 8 servings.

Approx Per Serving: Cal 442; Prot 6 g;
Carbo 29 g; Fiber 4 g; T Fat 36 g;
Chol 23 mg; Sod 304 mg.

Dawn Hopper
West Blocton High School
West Blocton, Alabama

BROCCOLI AND SWISS CHEESE SALAD

1 large bunch broccoli,
  chopped
1/4 cup chopped Swiss cheese
10 mushrooms, sliced
1/2 cup raisins
1/2 cup chopped red onion
1/4 cup sunflower seed
10 slices crisp-fried bacon,
  crumbled
1 cup mayonnaise-type salad
  dressing
2 tablespoons vinegar
1/2 cup sugar

Combine broccoli, cheese, mushrooms, raisins, onion, sunflower seed and bacon in bowl; mix well. Combine salad dressing, vinegar and sugar in small bowl; mix well. Add to salad; toss gently. Chill for 1 to 3 hours. Yield: 10 servings.

Approx Per Serving: Cal 240; Prot 6 g; Carbo 26 g; Fiber 2 g; T Fat 14 g; Chol 14 mg; Sod 287 mg.

Sharlene Lohmann Book
Oxford High School
Oxford, Kansas

BROCCOLI AND MUSHROOM SALAD

1/3 cup olive oil
1 tablespoon sesame oil
1 tablespoon soy sauce
2 tablespoons lemon juice
1/3 cup rice wine vinegar
6 cloves of garlic, crushed
1 tablespoon minced
  gingerroot
1 teaspoon salt
12 ounces fresh mushrooms,
  cut into quarters
2 pounds fresh broccoli
1 1/2 cups toasted walnut
  halves

Combine olive oil, sesame oil, soy sauce, lemon juice, vinegar, garlic, gingerroot and salt in bowl with airtight lid; mix well. Add mushrooms; cover. Marinate for 6 hours or longer, turning or shaking bowl frequently. Cut broccoli into 3 to 4-inch spears. Steam just until tender-crisp; rinse with cold water. Chill in refrigerator. Add broccoli to mushrooms; mix well. Let stand for 15 minutes. Sprinkle with walnuts.
Yield: 8 servings.

Approx Per Serving: Cal 288; Prot 8 g; Carbo 14 g; Fiber 6 g; T Fat 25 g; Chol 0 mg; Sod 431 mg.

Merri McKenzie
Suwannee High School
Live Oak, Florida

 Chill onions before chopping to prevent watery eyes!

BROCCOLI SALAD

4 cups chopped broccoli
2 carrots, chopped
2 cups chopped cauliflower
1 small red onion, chopped
¼ cup raisins
8 slices crisp-fried bacon,
  crumbled
1 cup mayonnaise
3 tablespoons white vinegar
¼ cup sugar

Combine broccoli, carrots, cauliflower, onion, raisins and bacon in bowl; mix well. Combine mayonnaise, vinegar and sugar in small bowl; mix until smooth. Add to vegetables; toss to mix well. May use reduced-calorie mayonnaise and artificial sweetener if preferred. Yield: 8 servings.

*Approx Per Serving: Cal 304; Prot 5 g;
Carbo 18 g; Fiber 3 g; T Fat 25 g;
Chol 22 mg; Sod 280 mg.*

*Sandra S. Schauble
West Caldwell High School
Lenoir, North Carolina*

CRUNCHY HAWAIIAN SALAD

½ cup oil
1 tablespoon sesame oil
6 tablespoons vinegar
¼ cup sugar
Salt to taste
1 teaspoon pepper
1 head cabbage, shredded
4 green onions, chopped
1 11-ounce can mandarin
  oranges, drained
1 3-ounce package ramen
  noodles
¼ cup slivered almonds,
  toasted
¼ cup sesame seed, toasted

Combine oil, sesame oil, vinegar, sugar, salt and pepper in small bowl; mix well. Chill in refrigerator. Combine cabbage, green onions and mandarin oranges in bowl; mix well. Reserve seasoning packet from noodles for another use; crumble noodles into salad. Sprinkle with almonds and sesame seed. Add dressing; toss to mix well. Yield: 12 servings.

*Approx Per Serving: Cal 215; Prot 3 g;
Carbo 18 g; Fiber 3 g; T Fat 15 g;
Chol 0 mg; Sod 192 mg.*

*Janet M. Brooks
Grace E. Metz Junior High School
Manassas, Virginia*

 *Fresh lemon juice or wine vinegars sprinkled over fresh vegetables
enhance the flavors so that other dressings are hardly necessary.*

CHINESE SLAW

1/4 cup wine vinegar
1/4 cup oil
2 tablespoons sugar
1   3-ounce package
     chicken-flavored ramen
     noodles
Salt and pepper to taste
1/2 head cabbage, shredded
4 green onions, chopped
3 tablespoons sunflower seed

Combine vinegar, oil, sugar, flavoring packet from noodles, salt and pepper in jar; shake to mix well. Combine cabbage, green onions and sunflower seed in salad bowl. Crumble noodles into salad. Add dressing. Let stand for 5 minutes. Yield: 6 servings.

Approx Per Serving: Cal 229; Prot 4 g; Carbo 22 g; Fiber 3 g; T Fat 15 g; Chol 0 mg; Sod 374 mg.

Linda McCabe
Shelbyville High School
Shelbyville, Illinois

MARINATED CABBAGE SLAW

1 head cabbage, shredded
1 onion, grated
1/2 cup grated green bell
     pepper
1 cup sugar
3/4 cup oil
1 cup white vinegar
1 teaspoon mustard seed
1 teaspoon celery seed
1 teaspoon salt

Layer cabbage, onion and green pepper in salad bowl. Sprinkle with sugar. Bring oil, vinegar, mustard seed, celery seed and salt to a boil in saucepan. Pour over layers. Chill for 4 hours to overnight. Yield: 12 servings.

Approx Per Serving: Cal 198; Prot <1 g; Carbo 20 g; Fiber 1 g; T Fat 14 g; Chol 0 mg; Sod 183 mg.

Joette Tribble
Martins Mill Independent School District
Ben Wheeler, Texas

 Add interest to cabbage salad by adding 1/4 to 1/3 package broken dry ramen noodles just before serving.

REALLY DIFFERENT SLAW

2 cups oil
3/4 cup rice vinegar
1/2 cup sugar
1 teaspoon salt
1 teaspoon pepper
1/2 cup sliced almonds
1/2 cup sesame seed
1 head cabbage, chopped
6 green onions, finely
    chopped
2　3-ounce packages ramen
    noodles

Combine oil, vinegar, sugar, salt and pepper in bowl; mix well. Toast almonds and sesame seed until light brown, stirring often. Combine cabbage and green onions in large salad bowl. Reserve flavor packet from noodles for another use. Crumble noodles into salad. Add toasted almonds, sesame seed and dressing; mix well. May store in refrigerator for several days.
Yield: 12 servings.

Approx Per Serving: Cal 523; Prot 6 g; Carbo 27 g; Fiber 4 g; T Fat 45 g; Chol 0 mg; Sod 554 mg.

Carolyn Stokes Buchanan
Batesville High School
Batesville, Arkansas

COPPER PENNY SALAD

2 pounds carrots
1 medium green bell pepper,
    chopped
2 medium onions, chopped
1　10-ounce can tomato soup
2/3 cup sugar
1/2 cup oil
1 teaspoon mustard
3/4 cup vinegar
1 teaspoon Worcestershire
    sauce
1/2 teaspoon salt

Peel and slice carrots. Cook in water to just cover in saucepan until tender-crisp; drain. Combine with green pepper and onions in bowl; mix well. Combine soup, sugar, oil, mustard, vinegar, Worcestershire sauce and salt in saucepan. Heat until sugar dissolves. Pour over salad; mix well. Chill overnight.
Yield: 12 servings.

Approx Per Serving: Cal 185; Prot 2 g; Carbo 25 g; Fiber 3 g; T Fat 10 g; Chol 0 mg; Sod 290 mg.

Linda Wattles
Gillespie High School
Gillespie, Illinois

 To keep lettuce longer and fresher, wrap cleaned lettuce in moist paper towels and refrigerate.

ORANGE AND CARROT SALAD

1 6-ounce package orange
    gelatin
1 cup grated carrots
1 cup chopped pecans
2 cups whipped topping
1/4 cup shredded Cheddar
    cheese

Prepare gelatin using package directions. Chill until partially set. Add carrots and pecans. Spoon into dish. Spread with whipped topping; sprinkle with cheese. Yield: 8 servings.

Approx Per Serving: Cal 258; Prot 4 g;
Carbo 27 g; Fiber 1 g; T Fat 16 g;
Chol 4 mg; Sod 99 mg.

Judy Fletcher
Decatur High School
Decatur, Arkansas

SUNSHINE SALAD

1 3-ounce package lemon
    gelatin
1 cup boiling water
12 large marshmallows
2 stalks celery, chopped
2 carrots, grated
1 cup crushed pineapple
1 cup mayonnaise
12 ounces whipped topping
1 cup cottage cheese
1/2 cup chopped pecans

Dissolve gelatin in boiling water in bowl. Stir in marshmallows until dissolved. Add celery, carrots and pineapple. Fold in remaining ingredients. Spoon into 9x13-inch dish. Chill. Yield: 15 servings.

Approx Per Serving: Cal 275; Prot 3 g;
Carbo 21 g; Fiber 1 g; T Fat 21 g;
Chol 11 mg; Sod 177 mg.

Bonnie Claycomb
Caverna High School
Horse Cave, Kentucky

CAULIFLOWER AND BROCCOLI SALAD

1 cup mayonnaise
2 tablespoons oil
2 tablespoons vinegar
2 tablespoons sugar
1 bunch green onions, chopped
Salt and pepper to taste
1 bunch broccoli, chopped
1 head cauliflower, chopped
1 medium tomato, chopped

Combine first 7 ingredients in bowl; mix well. Combine broccoli, cauliflower and tomato in bowl with airtight cover. Add dressing; toss to mix well. Chill, covered, for 8 hours, stirring occasionally. Yield: 8 servings.

Approx Per Serving: Cal 270; Prot 3 g;
Carbo 10 g; Fiber 3 g; T Fat 26 g;
Chol 16 mg; Sod 177 mg.

Sundra Ingram
Lineville High School
Lineville, Alabama

CAULIFLOWER CONFETTI SALAD

1 medium head cauliflower,
  chopped
1 bunch broccoli, chopped
2 small onions, sliced into
  rings
3 stalks celery, chopped
1/4 cup sliced stuffed olives
1/2 cup chopped green bell
  pepper
1/2 cup mayonnaise
1/3 cup Italian salad dressing
1 teaspoon sugar
1/2 teaspoon salt
1/4 teaspoon pepper

Combine cauliflower, broccoli, onions, celery, olives and green pepper in salad bowl; mix well. Mix mayonnaise, salad dressing, sugar, salt and pepper in small bowl. Add to salad; toss gently to mix. Chill, covered, for 3 to 4 hours.
Yield: 10 servings.

Approx Per Serving: Cal 154; Prot 2 g; Carbo 8 g; Fiber 3 g; T Fat 15 g; Chol 7 mg; Sod 370 mg.

Hazel C. Moore
George Washington High School
Danville, Virginia

CHRISTMAS VEGETABLE SALAD

Flowerets of 1 bunch broccoli
Flowerets of 1 head
  cauliflower
1 red bell pepper, coarsely
  chopped
1 medium red onion,
  chopped
1   8-ounce bottle of Italian
  salad dressing
Freshly ground pepper to
  taste

Steam broccoli in saucepan for 2 minutes or until tender-crisp. Rinse immediately in ice water. Combine with cauliflower, red pepper and onion in bowl with airtight lid. Add salad dressing and pepper; mix well. Chill, covered, for 24 hours or longer, stirring occasionally. Serve in lettuce-lined salad bowl.
Yield: 8 servings.

Approx Per Serving: Cal 166; Prot 3 g; Carbo 10 g; Fiber 3 g; T Fat 17 g; Chol 0 mg; Sod 159 mg.

Jean S. Lewis
Princess Anne High School
Virginia Beach, Virginia

 To save refrigerator space and speed salad making, peel and cut fresh vegetables and store in airtight plastic bags.

CAULIFLOWER SALAD

Flowerets of 1 head
  cauliflower
1 cup sliced radishes
6 green onions, chopped
1 cup sour cream
1 cup mayonnaise-type salad
  dressing
1 envelope cheese-garlic
  salad dressing mix
2 tablespoons parsley flakes

Combine cauliflower, radishes and green onions in salad bowl. Add mixture of remaining ingredients; mix well. Chill, covered, until serving time. Yield: 12 servings.

Approx Per Serving: Cal 101; Prot 2 g;
Carbo 7 g; Fiber 2 g; T Fat 8 g;
Chol 13 mg; Sod 119 mg.
Nutritional information does not include
salad dressing mix.

Pat Vaughan
Fairfield High School
Fairfield, Illinois

CAULIFLOWER AND CHEDDAR SALAD

1 head cauliflower, chopped
8 green onions, chopped
8 ounces Cheddar cheese,
  cubed
1   8-ounce bottle of ranch
  salad dressing

Combine vegetables and cheese in salad bowl. Add salad dressing; toss to mix. Yield: 10 servings.

Approx Per Serving: Cal 187; Prot 7 g;
Carbo 4 g; Fiber 1 g; T Fat 16 g;
Chol 33 mg; Sod 246 mg.

Sally Gibson Hennard
Wickes High School
Wickes, Arkansas

PARMESAN CAULIFLOWER SALAD

1 head lettuce, chopped
1 purple onion, sliced into
  rings
1 pound bacon, crisp-fried,
  crumbled
Flowerets of 1 head
  cauliflower
2 cups mayonnaise
1/3 cup Parmesan cheese
1/4 cup sugar
Salt and pepper to taste

Layer lettuce, onion, bacon and cauliflower in large salad bowl. Spread mixture of remaining ingredients over layers, sealing to edge of bowl. Chill, covered, overnight. Toss at serving time. Yield: 12 servings.

Approx Per Serving: Cal 369; Prot 6 g;
Carbo 8 g; Fiber 1 g; T Fat 36 g;
Chol 33 mg; Sod 437 mg.

Sandi Taylor
Lakeside High School
Evans, Georgia

ITALIAN CHICK-PEA SALAD

1 6-ounce envelope Italian
   salad dressing mix
1/4 cup cider vinegar
1 9-ounce package frozen
   Italian green beans,
   cooked, drained
1 16-ounce can chick-peas,
   drained
1 7-ounce can pitted olives,
   drained
1 cup sliced celery
1 small red onion, thinly
   sliced
1/2 cup mayonnaise

Combine salad dressing mix and vinegar in medium bowl; mix well. Add green beans, chick-peas, olives, celery and onion; toss to coat well. Chill, covered, overnight. Toss salad with mayonnaise just before serving. Yield: 8 servings.

Approx Per Serving: Cal 270; Prot 6 g; Carbo 26 g; Fiber 6 g; T Fat 18 g; Chol 8 mg; Sod 1488 mg.

Mary Jane Brooks
Girard High School
Girard, Ohio

CHEESY CORN BREAD SALAD

2 7-ounce packages corn
   bread mix
1 medium onion, chopped
1 medium green bell pepper,
   chopped
3 radishes, chopped
1/4 cup chopped olives
1/2 7-ounce can water
   chestnuts, chopped
1/4 cup chopped sweet pickles
2 tomatoes, peeled and
   chopped
1/2 cup chopped celery
1 1/2 cups shredded Cheddar
   cheese
2 hard-boiled eggs, chopped
Minced garlic, salt and
   pepper to taste
1 1/2 cups mayonnaise-type
   salad dressing
1/3 cup milk

Prepare and bake corn bread using package directions. Cool to room temperature. Crumble into bowl. Combine onion, green pepper, radishes, olives, water chestnuts, sweet pickles, tomatoes, celery, cheese and eggs in bowl; mix gently. Season with garlic, salt and pepper. Mix salad dressing and milk in small bowl. Layer corn bread, vegetable mixture and salad dressing 1/3 at a time in salad bowl. Yield: 12 servings.

Approx Per Serving: Cal 363; Prot 9 g; Carbo 35 g; Fiber 3 g; T Fat 23 g; Chol 101 mg; Sod 679 mg.

Kristi Berner
East Newton High School
Granby, Missouri

MEXICAN CORN BREAD SALAD

1 7-ounce package Mexican
   corn bread mix
1 small sweet purple onion,
   finely chopped
1 16-ounce can Mexicorn,
   drained
2 tomatoes, chopped
1/2 cup shredded Cheddar
   cheese
1/3 cup mayonnaise

Prepare corn bread using package directions; cool and crumble. Combine with remaining ingredients in salad bowl; mix lightly. Chill until serving time. Yield: 10 servings.

*Approx Per Serving: Cal 207; Prot 5 g;
Carbo 24 g; Fiber 2 g; T Fat 12 g;
Chol 35 mg; Sod 358 mg.*

*Judy F. Honey
Arkadelphia High School
Arkadelphia, Arkansas*

COLD CORN SALAD

1/2 cup sour cream
1/2 cup mayonnaise
1 teaspoon vinegar
Salt to taste
2 16-ounce cans corn,
   drained
1/2 green bell pepper,
   chopped
1/2 cucumber, chopped
6 green onions, chopped

Combine sour cream, mayonnaise, vinegar and salt in small bowl; mix well. Combine remaining ingredients in salad bowl. Add dressing; mix well. Chill for 3 hours. Yield: 8 servings.

*Approx Per Serving: Cal 226; Prot 4 g;
Carbo 23 g; Fiber 2 g; T Fat 15 g;
Chol 15 mg; Sod 349 mg.*

*Jan Knuth
Southeast High School
Wichita, Kansas*

CORN SALAD

1 16-ounce can Shoe Peg
   corn, drained
1/2 cup chopped celery
1/2 cup chopped sweet pickles
1/2 cup chopped green bell
   pepper
1/2 cup chopped onion
1/2 cup chopped carrots
3 hard-boiled eggs, chopped
Salt and pepper to taste
1/2 cup (about) mayonnaise

Combine corn, celery, pickles, green pepper, onion, carrots and eggs in salad bowl; mix well. Season with salt and pepper. Add mayonnaise; mix lightly. Yield: 6 servings.

*Approx Per Serving: Cal 138; Prot 6 g;
Carbo 24 g; Fiber 2 g; T Fat 4 g;
Chol 106 mg; Sod 357 mg.*

*Emily Lewis
Capitol Hill High School
Oklahoma City, Oklahoma*

COMPANY CUCUMBER SALAD

3 large cucumbers, peeled,
  thinly sliced
1/4 teaspoon salt
1/2 cup plain yogurt
1/2 cup sour cream
1/3 cup mayonnaise
4 teaspoons wine vinegar
1/4 cup chopped green onions
1 tablespoon minced fresh
  parsley
1 clove of garlic, minced
Pepper to taste

Sprinkle cucumbers with salt. Let stand for 15 minutes. Drain well on paper towels. Combine yogurt, sour cream, mayonnaise, vinegar, green onions, parsley, garlic and pepper in small bowl; mix well. Place cucumbers in serving bowl. Add dressing; toss gently. Chill, covered, for 2 hours or longer. Yield: 6 servings.

Approx Per Serving: Cal 162; Prot 3 g;
Carbo 8 g; Fiber 2 g; T Fat 14 g;
Chol 17 mg; Sod 185 mg.

Anne VanBeber
L.V. Berkner High School
Richardson, Texas

CUCUMBER SALAD

4 cucumbers, thinly sliced
1 tablespoon salt
1 medium onion, sliced
1 tablespoon white vinegar
1 cup sour cream
Pepper to taste

Layer cucumbers in bowl, sprinkling each layer with salt. Add onion. Let stand for 3 hours, stirring occasionally. Drain well. Add vinegar, sour cream and pepper; mix well. Chill overnight. Yield: 8 servings.

Approx Per Serving: Cal 88; Prot 2 g;
Carbo 7 g; Fiber 2 g; T Fat 6 g;
Chol 13 mg; Sod 818 mg.

Sandra Huffman
River Wood High School
Atlanta, Georgia

 To keep lettuce crisp and fresh, break it up into an airtight bowl (with lid), place a paper towel over bowl, and cover with lid (leave towel hanging out of edges). Place bowl in refrigerator lid side down. Lettuce will keep for several days.

TURKISH CUCUMBER SALAD

3 large cucumbers
3 large tomatoes
2 tablespoons salt
4 bunches fresh dillweed
4 to 6 cloves of garlic,
  crushed
1 cup plain yogurt
1/4 cup olive oil
Several drops of water
Chili powder to taste
8 Turkish black olives

Peel cucumbers and slice into quarters lengthwise, discarding seed. Slice quarters into bite-sized pieces. Peel and seed tomatoes; chop into bite-sized pieces. Combine with cucumbers in bowl. Add salt; mix well. Chill for 1 hour. Reserve several sprigs of dillweed for garnish. Chop remaining dillweed. Combine chopped dillweed with garlic, yogurt, olive oil and enough water to make of desired consistency in bowl. Add to cucumber mixture; mix gently. Chill for 2 hours. Drain well. Serve on lettuce-lined serving plate. Sprinkle with chili powder; top with black olives. Garnish with mint and reserved dillweed. Yield: 8 servings.

Approx Per Serving: Cal 112; Prot 3 g;
Carbo 8 g; Fiber 2 g; T Fat 8 g;
Chol 2 mg; Sod 1661 mg.
Nutritional information includes
entire amount of marinade.

Nancy McIlvaine
Adena High School
Frankfort, Ohio

MOCK CAESAR SALAD

1/4 cup olive oil
1/4 cup white Worcestershire
  sauce
1 tablespoon lemon juice
1 teaspoon Dijon mustard
3 tablespoons Parmesan
  cheese
1 head romaine lettuce, torn
1 cup croutons
1/4 teaspoon pepper
1 tablespoon Parmesan
  cheese

Combine olive oil, Worcestershire sauce, lemon juice, mustard and 3 tablespoons cheese in salad bowl. Add lettuce and croutons; mix well. Sprinkle with pepper and 1 tablespoon cheese. Serve immediately. Yield: 6 servings.

Approx Per Serving: Cal 129; Prot 3 g;
Carbo 7 g; Fiber 1 g; T Fat 10 g;
Chol 3 mg; Sod 241 mg.

Cindy Matney
Grundy Senior High School
Grundy, Virginia

GREENS WITH ORANGE VINAIGRETTE

1 head romaine lettuce
12 ounces spinach
Sections of 1 large pink or
   red grapefruit
Sections of 1 large orange
1 large avocado, sliced
1 small red onion, thinly
   sliced
1/2 cup salted roasted peanuts
Orange Vinaigrette (page 122)

Tear romaine and spinach into bite-sized pieces. Combine with grapefruit, orange, avocado, onion and peanuts in bowl. Add Orange Vinaigrette; toss lightly. Yield: 10 servings.

Approx Per Serving: Cal 205; Prot 4 g;
Carbo 10 g; Fiber 5 g; T Fat 18 g;
Chol 0 mg; Sod 63 mg.

Linda Wahlberg
Franklin County High School
Rocky Mount, Virginia

LAYERED SALAD

1 head lettuce, torn
2 bunches spinach, torn
1 bunch green onions,
   chopped
6 hard-boiled eggs, chopped
1 10-ounce package frozen
   green peas
1 pound bacon, crisp-fried,
   crumbled
1 pound Swiss cheese, sliced
   into thin strips
1 cup mayonnaise

Layer lettuce, spinach, green onions, eggs, peas, bacon and cheese in large salad bowl. Spread mayonnaise over layers, sealing to edge of bowl. Chill, covered, overnight. Toss at serving time. Yield: 12 servings.

Approx Per Serving: Cal 405; Prot 20 g;
Carbo 7 g; Fiber 2 g; T Fat 34 g;
Chol 161 mg; Sod 461 mg.

Deborah R. Dykes
Stockbridge Junior High School
Stockbridge, Georgia

LAYERED SALAD WITH AVOCADO

1 head lettuce, torn
1 onion, chopped
1/2 cup chopped avocado
1 10-ounce package frozen
   green peas
2 cups ranch salad dressing
1 cup shredded Cheddar
   cheese
8 slices crisp-fried bacon,
   crumbled

Layer lettuce, onion, avocado and peas in 9x13-inch dish. Spread layers with salad dressing, sealing to edge of dish. Sprinkle with cheese and bacon. Chill overnight. Yield: 10 servings.

Approx Per Serving: Cal 297; Prot 8 g;
Carbo 9 g; Fiber 3 g; T Fat 26 g;
Chol 35 mg; Sod 395 mg.

Tammy J. Hall
Humble Middle School
Humble, Texas

ROMAINE SALAD WITH MANDARIN ORANGES

1 large head romaine lettuce,
  torn
4 small onions, thinly sliced
1 11-ounce can mandarin
  oranges, drained
2/3 cup oil
1/2 cup vinegar
1/2 cup sugar
1 teaspoon mustard
1 tablespoon poppy seed
1 teaspoon salt

Combine romaine lettuce, onions and mandarin oranges in salad bowl. Combine oil, vinegar, sugar, mustard, poppy seed and salt in jar; cover tightly. Shake to mix well. Add dressing to salad at serving time; toss gently. Yield: 8 servings.

Approx Per Serving: Cal 258; Prot 1 g;
Carbo 25 g; Fiber 2 g; T Fat 18 g;
Chol 0 mg; Sod 273 mg.

Linda Honaker
Glenwood Junior High School
Princeton, West Virginia

MANDARIN ORANGE TOSSED SALAD

1/4 cup wine vinegar
1/2 cup oil
1 tablespoon sugar
Salt and pepper to taste
3 3/4 ounces slivered almonds
2 tablespoons sugar
1 head lettuce, chopped
1/2 cup chopped green onions
  with tops
1/4 cup chopped celery
1 11-ounce can mandarin
  oranges, drained

Combine vinegar, oil, 1 tablespoon sugar, salt and pepper in bowl; mix well. Combine almonds with 2 tablespoons sugar in cast-iron skillet. Cook over low heat until sugar melts and almonds are coated and light brown, stirring constantly. Cool to room temperature. Combine lettuce, green onions, celery, mandarin oranges and caramelized almonds in salad bowl. Add dressing at serving time, tossing gently to mix well. Yield: 4 servings.

Approx Per Serving: Cal 495; Prot 6 g;
Carbo 31 g; Fiber 6 g; T Fat 41 g;
Chol 0 mg; Sod 20 mg.

Kay Mardis
Arab High School
Arab, Alabama

 When making guacamole, combine equal parts mashed ripe avocado and a colorful, fat-free mix of chopped tomato, chopped onion, cilantro and picante sauce to keep it light and to reduce fat.

ORANGE AND GREEN DELIGHT

1 head lettuce, torn
1 red onion, sliced into rings
3 oranges, peeled, chopped
1 cup dry-roasted peanuts
1   8-ounce bottle of Italian
    salad dressing
2 teaspoons sugar

Combine lettuce, onion, oranges and peanuts in salad bowl. Combine salad dressing and sugar in small bowl; mix well. Add to salad; toss to mix. May substitute spinach for any or all of the lettuce. Yield: 12 servings.

*Approx Per Serving: Cal 182; Prot 4 g;
Carbo 10 g; Fiber 2 g; T Fat 17 g;
Chol 0 mg; Sod 96 mg.*

*Alice Schleg
Grayslake Community High School
Grayslake, Illinois*

OVERNIGHT SALAD

1 head lettuce, chopped
1 onion, finely chopped
5 stalks celery, thinly sliced
1   10-ounce package frozen
    green peas
2 cups mayonnaise
2 tablespoons sugar
1/2 cup bacon bits
2 hard-boiled eggs, chopped
1/2 cup shredded Cheddar
    cheese

Combine lettuce, onion, celery and peas in salad bowl; mix well. Mix mayonnaise and sugar in small bowl. Spread over salad, sealing to edge of bowl. Chill, tightly covered, for 8 hours or longer. Top with bacon bits, eggs and cheese. Yield: 10 servings.

*Approx Per Serving: Cal 418; Prot 5 g;
Carbo 12 g; Fiber 4 g; T Fat 40 g;
Chol 75 mg; Sod 483 mg.*

*Emma L. Wengert
Waldron High School
Waldron, Arkansas*

 On layered salads calling for mayonnaise, sprinkle about 1 tablespoon sugar over the mayonnaise to add a taste similiar to a salad dressing.

TWENTY-FOUR HOUR VEGETABLE SALAD

6 cups chopped lettuce
3 hard-boiled eggs, sliced
1 teaspoon sugar
¼ teaspoon salt
¼ teaspoon pepper
1 10-ounce package frozen
    green peas, thawed
2 cups cauliflowerets
8 ounces bacon, crisp-fried,
    crumbled
2 cups shredded Swiss cheese
1 cup mayonnaise
¼ cup sliced green onions
Paprika to taste
¼ cup Parmesan cheese

Layer half the lettuce and all the eggs in large salad bowl, sprinkling layers with sugar, salt and pepper. Layer peas, cauliflower, remaining lettuce, bacon and Swiss cheese over eggs. Spread mayonnaise over layers, sealing to edge of bowl. Chill, covered, for 24 hours. Top with green onions, paprika and Parmesan cheese. Toss at serving time. Yield: 15 servings.

Approx Per Serving: Cal 232; Prot 9 g;
Carbo 5 g; Fiber 2 g; T Fat 20 g;
Chol 70 mg; Sod 295 mg.

Jean Newman
Cosgrove Junior High School
Spencerport, New York

FRESH MUSHROOM SALAD

1 pound fresh mushrooms,
    sliced
1 small bunch green onions,
    sliced
1 cup shredded Cheddar
    cheese
¼ cup oil
½ cup vinegar
2 tablespoons Greek
    seasoning

Combine mushrooms with green onions and cheese in salad bowl. Combine oil, vinegar and Greek seasoning in small bowl; mix well. Add to salad; mix gently. Let stand for 10 to 15 minutes, mixing several times. Yield: 8 servings.

Approx Per Serving: Cal 136; Prot 5 g;
Carbo 4 g; Fiber 1 g; T Fat 12 g;
Chol 15 mg; Sod 91 mg.
Nutritional information does not
include Greek seasoning.

Retha Asklund
Sasakwa High School
Sasakwa, Oklahoma

 Store rinsed lettuce in a zip-lock type bag in the refrigerator to save space and to keep lettuce crisp.

MUSHROOM AND ORANGE SALAD

1/4 cup slivered almonds
4 slices bacon
1 large head lettuce, torn
1   11-ounce can mandarin
    oranges, drained
Bleu Cheese Vinaigrette
    (page 121)
8 ounces mushrooms, sliced

Toast almonds in cast-iron skillet over low heat for 5 minutes or until light brown. Remove with slotted spoon. Fry bacon in same skillet until crisp; drain and crumble. Combine lettuce and oranges in large salad bowl. Add Bleu Cheese Vinaigrette, mushrooms, bacon and almonds; toss to mix well. May make in advance and chill until serving time. Yield: 12 servings.

*Approx Per Serving: Cal 125; Prot 3 g;
Carbo 6 g; Fiber 1 g; T Fat 11 g;
Chol 4 mg; Sod 132 mg.*

*M. Joanne Hughes
Shawnee Mission North High School
Shawnee Mission, Kansas*

LONE STAR CAVIAR

1 pound dried black-eyed
    peas
2 cups Italian salad dressing
2 cups chopped green bell
    peppers
1 1/2 cups chopped onions
1 cup finely chopped green
    onions
1/2 cup finely chopped
    jalapeño peppers
3 ounces pimento, chopped,
    drained
1 tablespoon finely chopped
    garlic
Hot pepper sauce to taste
Salt to taste

Soak peas in water to cover for 6 hours to overnight; drain well. Combine with fresh water to cover in saucepan. Bring to a boil over high heat; reduce heat. Simmer for 45 minutes or until tender; do not overcook. Drain well. Combine with salad dressing in large bowl. Add green peppers, onions, green onions, jalapeño peppers, pimento, garlic, pepper sauce and salt; mix well. Yield: 12 servings.

*Approx Per Serving: Cal 327; Prot 10 g;
Carbo 30 g; Fiber 12 g; T Fat 24 g;
Chol 0 mg; Sod 282 mg.*

*Elysce Garrison
Aldine Senior High School
Houston, Texas*

GREEN PEA SALAD

1 16-ounce can tiny green
   peas, drained
1 small onion, chopped
2 hard-boiled eggs, chopped
1 dill pickle, chopped
1 small carrot, chopped
1 cup cubed Cheddar cheese
1 teaspoon salt
Pepper to taste
1/4 cup (or more) mayonnaise-
   type salad dressing

Combine peas, onion, eggs, pickle, carrot and cheese in small bowl. Season with salt and pepper. Add salad dressing; toss lightly to mix. Yield: 4 servings.

Approx Per Serving: Cal 308; Prot 16 g;
Carbo 23 g; Fiber 7 g; T Fat 18 g;
Chol 140 mg; Sod 1287 mg.

Rhonda White
Paris High School
Paris, Arkansas

PEA AND GREEN BEAN SALAD

1/2 cup vinegar
1/4 cup oil
1 tablespoon water
3/4 cup sugar
1 tablespoon salt
Paprika to taste
1 16-ounce can tiny green
   peas, drained
1 16-ounce can French-style
   green beans, drained
2 stalks celery, chopped
1/2 green bell pepper, chopped
1/2 onion, sliced
1 2-ounce jar chopped pimento

Combine vinegar, oil, water, sugar, salt and paprika in small bowl; mix well. Combine remaining ingredients in salad bowl. Add dressing; mix well. Marinate in refrigerator for 24 hours. Drain 30 minutes before serving. Yield: 8 servings.

Approx Per Serving: Cal 193; Prot 3 g;
Carbo 31 g; Fiber 4 g; T Fat 7 g;
Chol 0 mg; Sod 1076 mg.
Nutritional information includes
entire amount of marinade.

Phyllis Cowan
Harrison Junior High School
Harrison, Arkansas

PEA-NUT SALAD

1 10-ounce package frozen
   green peas, thawed
1/2 cup unsalted peanuts
1/2 cup mayonnaise

Combine peas and peanuts in bowl. Add mayonnaise; mix well. Yield: 6 servings.

Approx Per Serving: Cal 236; Prot 6 g;
Carbo 9 g; Fiber 3 g; T Fat 21 g;
Chol 11 mg; Sod 159 mg.

Ramona Lawton
Flat Rock Junior High School
East Flat Rock, North Carolina

COTTAGE CHEESE POTATO SALAD

10 medium potatoes, peeled, sliced
Salt and pepper to taste
2 cups small curd cream-style cottage cheese
1 cup mayonnaise
1 medium red onion, sliced into rings
Paprika to taste

Cook potatoes in water to cover in saucepan just until tender; do not overcook. Drain well. Arrange half the potatoes in 4-quart bowl. Sprinkle with salt and pepper. Spread with half the cottage cheese and mayonnaise, mixing with spoon. Top with half the onion rings. Repeat layers; sprinkle with paprika. Yield: 12 servings.

Approx Per Serving: Cal 293; Prot 7 g; Carbo 30 g; Fiber 2 g; T Fat 16 g; Chol 16 mg; Sod 253 mg.

Carolyn Cotton
Bristow High School
Bristow, Oklahoma

GERMAN POTATO SALAD

8 medium potatoes
6 slices bacon
1 cup chopped scallions
2 tablespoons flour
1 tablespoon sugar
1 teaspoon celery seed
1/2 cup Italian salad dressing
Vinegar to taste
1 1/2 teaspoons salt
Pepper to taste

Cook potatoes in water to cover in saucepan for 25 to 30 minutes or until tender; drain. Peel and slice potatoes. Fry bacon in large skillet. Drain and crumble bacon, reserving 1/4 cup drippings. Sauté scallions in reserved drippings. Stir in flour, sugar, celery seed, salad dressing, vinegar, salt, pepper and enough water to make of desired consistency. Cook until thickened, stirring constantly. Cook for 1 to 2 minutes longer. Add potatoes and bacon. Heat to serving temperature, stirring gently. Yield: 8 servings.

Approx Per Serving: Cal 332; Prot 7 g; Carbo 56 g; Fiber 5 g; T Fat 11 g; Chol 4 mg; Sod 564 mg.

Lucile P. Sprinkle
Madison High School
Marshall, North Carolina

LAYERED POTATO SALAD

1¹/₂ cups mayonnaise
1 cup sour cream
1¹/₂ teaspoons horseradish
1 teaspoon celery seed
¹/₂ teaspoon salt
1 cup chopped fresh parsley
2 medium onions, minced
8 medium whole potatoes,
  cooked
2 tablespoons chopped
  pimento

Combine mayonnaise, sour cream, horseradish, celery seed and salt in bowl; mix well. Mix parsley and onions in small bowl. Cut potatoes into thick slices. Alternate layers of potatoes, mayonnaise mixture and onion mixture in large serving bowl until all ingredients are used, sprinkling potatoes lightly with additional salt. Top with pimento. Chill, covered, overnight. Yield: 10 servings.

Approx Per Serving: Cal 476; Prot 5 g; Carbo 46 g; Fiber 5 g; T Fat 31 g; Chol 30 mg; Sod 323 mg.

Rebecca Carabelas
Shawnee Mission North School
Shawnee Mission, Kansas

LEAN POTATO SALAD

4 medium potatoes
¹/₂ cup chopped green bell
  pepper
3 tablespoons chopped onion
8 stuffed olives, sliced
Whites of 3 hard-boiled
  eggs, chopped
¹/₄ teaspoon celery salt
¹/₄ teaspoon onion salt
¹/₄ cup plain low-fat yogurt
1 tablespoon Dijon mustard

Cook unpeeled potatoes in water to cover in saucepan until tender. Drain and chop potatoes. Combine with green pepper, onion, olives, egg whites, celery salt and onion salt in salad bowl; mix well. Add yogurt and mustard; mix gently. Serve immediately. Yield: 6 servings.

Approx Per Serving: Cal 172; Prot 6 g; Carbo 36 g; Fiber 4 g; T Fat 1 g; Chol 1 mg; Sod 378 mg.

Linda Townes
Isabella High School
Maplesville, Alabama

 When cooking vegetables for salads, start those that grow under the ground such as carrots, potatoes or beets in cold water. Anything that grows above the ground such as peas, beans or broccoli should be started in boiling water.

SOUR CREAM POTATO SALAD

7 medium potatoes
1/3 cup low-calorie Italian
  salad dressing
3/4 cup chopped celery
1/3 cup minced green onions
4 hard-boiled eggs, finely
  chopped
1 cup mayonnaise
1/2 cup low-fat sour cream
11/2 teaspoons prepared
  mustard
Celery seed and salt to taste

Cook unpeeled potatoes in water to cover in saucepan until tender; drain. Peel and chop potatoes. Combine with Italian dressing in bowl while still warm; mix gently. Chill for 2 hours. Add celery, green onions and eggs. Mix mayonnaise, sour cream and mustard in small bowl. Add to salad; mix gently. Season with celery seed and salt. Chill for 2 hours longer. Yield: 8 servings.

Approx Per Serving: Cal 413; Prot 7 g;
Carbo 35 g; Fiber 3 g; T Fat 28 g;
Chol 123 mg; Sod 316 mg.

Carol Kerbel
O'Banion Middle School
Garland, Texas

FAVORITE RICE SALAD

1 cup brown rice, cooked
1/4 cup chopped onion
1 small green bell pepper,
  chopped
1 pimento, chopped
2 large tomatoes, chopped
1 tablespoon chopped parsley
1/4 cup oil
2 tablespoons wine vinegar
1/4 teaspoon Worcestershire
  sauce
1 clove of garlic, minced
1/2 teaspoon salt
1/8 teaspoon pepper

Combine rice, onion, green pepper, pimento, tomatoes and parsley in 11/2-quart salad bowl; mix well. Combine oil, vinegar, Worcestershire sauce, garlic, salt and pepper in small bowl; mix well. Add to salad; mix gently. Chill for 2 to 6 hours. Yield: 6 servings.

Approx Per Serving: Cal 208; Prot 3 g;
Carbo 28 g; Fiber 2 g; T Fat 10 g;
Chol 0 mg; Sod 187 mg.

Luana Ellis
Montesano High School
Montesano, Washington

 When buying leafy greens, avoid any that are oversized, spotted, limp or beginning to turn yellow; they're past their prime. Choose a head that gives slightly when squeezed and has good color—usually bright green.

LEMONY RICE SALAD

1½ cups uncooked long
   grain rice
1 tablespoon salt
4 quarts water
3 tablespoons lemon juice
¾ teaspoon grated lemon
   zest
6 tablespoons olive oil
Salt and pepper to taste
½ cup minced fresh parsley
3 scallions, thinly sliced
½ cup unsalted dry-roasted
   peanuts, coarsely chopped

Cook rice with 1 tablespoon salt in water in large saucepan for 10 minutes. Rinse and drain in colander. Place colander over saucepan of boiling water; cover with kitchen towel and lid. Steam for 15 minutes or until light and fluffy. Combine lemon juice, lemon zest, olive oil and salt and pepper to taste in bowl; whisk until smooth. Combine rice, parsley, scallions, peanuts and lemon dressing in serving bowl; mix gently. Chill, covered, for 3 hours or serve at room temperature. Yield: 6 servings.

*Approx Per Serving: Cal 253; Prot 5 g;
Carbo 16 g; Fiber 2 g; T Fat 20 g;
Chol 0 mg; Sod 1335 mg.*

*Jannie Barrington
Jones High School
Jones, Oklahoma*

RICE-A-RONI

1 7-ounce package
   chicken-flavored
   Rice-A-Roni
4 green onions, chopped
12 stuffed olives, sliced
2 6-ounce jars marinated
   artichoke hearts, drained
⅓ cup mayonnaise
¼ teaspoon curry powder

Prepare Rice-A-Roni using package directions. Cool to room temperature. Combine with green onions, olives, artichoke hearts, mayonnaise and curry powder in 2-quart bowl; mix well. Serve at room temperature. Yield: 6 servings.

*Approx Per Serving: Cal 277; Prot 4 g;
Carbo 29 g; Fiber 4 g; T Fat 17 g;
Chol 7 mg; Sod 962 mg.*

*JoAnn Vogelsang
Rockdale High School
Rockdale, Texas*

 A brown core in lettuce is a sign of oxidation and doesn't neces-sarily indicate poor quality. After lettuce is cut during harvesting, the core naturally browns as the cut surface seals to keep the head fresh and to hold in nutrients.

KRAUT SALAD

1   16-ounce can sauerkraut
1 cup chopped onion
1 green bell pepper, chopped
1   4-ounce jar chopped
    pimentos
2 cups chopped celery
1/2 cup vinegar
1/2 cup sugar

Combine sauerkraut, onion, green pepper, pimentos and celery in covered refrigerator bowl. Mix vinegar and sugar in small bowl. Add to salad; mix well. Chill, covered, for 24 hours to several days. May add chopped cucumbers if desired. Yield: 10 servings.

*Approx Per Serving: Cal 63; Prot 1 g;
Carbo 16 g; Fiber 2 g; T Fat <1 g;
Chol 0 mg; Sod 322 mg.*

*Suellen Ward
Guy-Perkins School
Guy, Arkansas*

SWEET SAUERKRAUT SALAD

2   16-ounce cans sauerkraut,
    drained
1 cup chopped celery
1   4-ounce jar chopped
    pimentos, drained
1 cup chopped green bell
    pepper
1 cup chopped purple onion
1   7-ounce can water
    chestnuts, drained,
    chopped
2/3 cup white vinegar
1/2 cup oil
1/3 cup water
11/4 cups sugar

Combine sauerkraut, celery, pimentos, green pepper, onion and water chestnuts in bowl with cover; mix well. Combine vinegar, oil, water and sugar in saucepan. Heat until sugar dissolves, stirring constantly. Pour over salad; mix well. Marinate, covered, in refrigerator for 3 hours to overnight. Yield: 12 servings.

*Approx Per Serving: Cal 195; Prot 1 g;
Carbo 29 g; Fiber 3 g; T Fat 9 g;
Chol 0 mg; Sod 512 mg.*

*Vickie Bruce
Lake Hamilton Junior High School
Pearcy, Arkansas*

Alfalfa sprouts will last longer if you wash only the amount needed rather than the whole container.

FRESH SPINACH SALAD

1 12-ounce package
  spinach, torn
1/2 medium onion, chopped
1 cup shredded Cheddar
  cheese
2 hard-boiled eggs, chopped
3 slices crisp-fried bacon,
  crumbled
1 cup mayonnaise-type salad
  dressing
1 tablespoon (or more) taco
  sauce
1 1/2 teaspoons horseradish
Salt and pepper to taste

Toss spinach with onion, cheese, eggs and bacon in salad bowl. Combine salad dressing, taco sauce, horseradish, salt and pepper in small bowl; mix well. Add to salad; toss to mix well. Yield: 6 servings.

Approx Per Serving: Cal 232; Prot 10 g; Carbo 10 g; Fiber 2 g; T Fat 18 g; Chol 103 mg; Sod 448 mg.

Patricia A. Parker
Cabool High School
Cabool, Missouri

KOREAN SALAD

16 ounces fresh spinach, torn
1 16-ounce can bean
  sprouts, rinsed, drained
1 7-ounce can water
  chestnuts, drained,
  chopped
3 hard-boiled eggs, sliced
4 ounces bacon, crisp-fried,
  crumbled
Korean Salad Dressing
  (page 118)

Combine spinach, bean sprouts, water chestnuts, eggs and bacon in salad bowl. Add Korean Salad Dressing; toss to mix well. Serve immediately. Yield: 10 servings.

Approx Per Serving: Cal 335; Prot 5 g; Carbo 24 g; Fiber 3 g; T Fat 25 g; Chol 67 mg; Sod 324 mg.

Pamela Cormany
Adena High School
Frankfort, Ohio

 Wash all salad greens under cold running water, pat dry, wrap loosely and refrigerate. Always tear salad greens into pieces with your hands. A knife will brown the edges.

SPINACH AND PECAN SALAD

1/4 cup pecans
1 tablespoon butter
2 12-ounce packages
   spinach, torn
4 ounces fresh mushrooms,
   sliced
1/2 cup sliced water chestnuts
1 cucumber, sliced
2 hard-boiled eggs, chopped
5 slices crisp-fried bacon,
   crumbled
1 8-ounce bottle of creamy
   Caesar salad dressing

Toast pecans in butter in skillet. Combine with spinach, mushrooms, water chestnuts, cucumber, eggs and bacon in salad bowl. Add salad dressing; toss to mix well. Let stand for 2 hours to improve flavor. Yield: 12 servings.

*Approx Per Serving: Cal 158; Prot 6 g;
Carbo 5 g; Fiber 3 g; T Fat 14 g;
Chol 63 mg; Sod 284 mg.*

*Denise Blanchard
Slaton High School
Slaton, Texas*

SPINACH SALAD

1/2 cup oil
1/4 cup catsup
2 tablespoons vinegar
1/3 cup sugar
1/4 cup finely chopped onion
1 1/2 teaspoons Worcestershire
   sauce
Salt to taste
16 ounces fresh spinach, torn
1 16-ounce can bean
   sprouts, drained
3 hard-boiled eggs, sliced
1 8-ounce can sliced water
   chestnuts, drained
6 slices crisp-fried bacon,
   crumbled

Combine oil, catsup, vinegar, sugar, onion, Worcestershire sauce and salt in jar; cover tightly. Shake until well mixed. Chill until serving time. Layer spinach, bean sprouts, eggs, water chestnuts and bacon 1/2 at a time in large bowl. Pour dressing over layers. Yield: 10 servings.

*Approx Per Serving: Cal 204; Prot 5 g;
Carbo 15 g; Fiber 3 g; T Fat 15 g;
Chol 67 mg; Sod 203 mg.*

*Linda Hyder
Flat Rock Junior High School
Hendersonville, North Carolina*

 Quick-chill individual bowls of tossed salad in the freezer for 30 seconds just before serving.

SPINACH AND APPLE SALAD

16 ounces fresh spinach, torn
1 bunch green onions,
   chopped
1 unpeeled apple, chopped
8 ounces bacon, crisp-fried,
   crumbled
2 hard-boiled eggs, chopped
1/3 cup mayonnaise
1/3 cup sour cream

Combine spinach, green onions, apple, bacon and eggs in salad bowl. Add mayonnaise and sour cream; toss to mix well. Chill until serving time. Yield: 8 servings.

*Approx Per Serving: Cal 180; Prot 6 g;
Carbo 6 g; Fiber 3 g; T Fat 15 g;
Chol 70 mg; Sod 255 mg.*

*Diane Sykes Talley
Plattsburg High School
Plattsburg, Missouri*

SPINACH SALAD WITH SPICY DRESSING

1 cup oil
1/4 cup vinegar
1/2 cup sugar
1/3 cup catsup
1 tablespoon Worcestershire
   sauce
1 small onion, chopped
1 teaspoon salt
8 ounces fresh spinach, torn
1/2 head lettuce, torn
3 hard-boiled eggs, chopped
1   16-ounce can bean
   sprouts, drained
1/2 cup crumbled crisp-fried
   bacon

Combine oil and vinegar in mixer bowl. Beat for 3 to 5 minutes. Add sugar, catsup, Worcestershire sauce, onion and salt; mix well. Chill until serving time. Combine spinach, lettuce, eggs, bean sprouts and bacon in salad bowl. Add dressing; toss to mix well. Yield: 8 servings.

*Approx Per Serving: Cal 381; Prot 6 g;
Carbo 20 g; Fiber 2 g; T Fat 32 g;
Chol 84 mg; Sod 534 mg.*

*Peggy Joy Glasgow
Fayette Middle School
Fayette, Alabama*

 To remove excess air from plastic bags when storing salad greens, insert straw at hand-gathered end of bag and suck out air. Close end tightly. Vegetables will keep for a much longer time.

SPRING SPINACH SALAD

2 tablespoons cider vinegar
1 tablespoon lemon juice
1 egg
1/2 teaspoon dry mustard
1/8 teaspoon paprika
Cayenne pepper to taste
1/2 teaspoon mixed tarragon,
  chervil, parsley and
  marjoram
1/2 teaspoon salt
Freshly ground pepper to
  taste
1 cup oil
1 10-ounce package fresh
  spinach, torn
3 slices crisp-fried bacon,
  crumbled
1 hard-boiled egg, chopped
1 hard-boiled egg, sliced

Whisk vinegar, lemon juice, egg, dry mustard, paprika, cayenne pepper, tarragon, chervil, parsley, marjoram, salt and pepper together in bowl. Whisk in oil. Store, tightly covered, in refrigerator for up to 5 days. Combine spinach, bacon and chopped egg in salad bowl. Add dressing; toss to mix well. Top with sliced egg. Yield: 4 servings.

*Approx Per Serving: Cal 586; Prot 8 g;
Carbo 4 g; Fiber 2 g; T Fat 61 g;
Chol 164 mg; Sod 450 mg.*

*Sharon Marich
Charlotte Wood Intermediate School
Danville, California*

FRUITED SPINACH SALAD

1 16-ounce can red cherries
  in vinegar
Juice of 2 oranges
Grated rind of 1 orange
Juice of 2 limes
Grated rind of 1 lime
1/2 cup olive oil
2 tablespoons chopped chives
1 12-ounce package fresh
  spinach, torn
Sections of 2 pink grapefruit
Sections of 4 oranges
4 pears, chopped

Drain cherries, reserving vinegar. Combine reserved vinegar with orange juice, orange rind, lime juice, lime rind, olive oil and chives in small bowl; whisk until well mixed. Place spinach in salad bowl. Arrange grapefruit sections, orange sections and pears on spinach. Drizzle with dressing. Top with cherries. Yield: 8 servings.

*Approx Per Serving: Cal 250; Prot 3 g;
Carbo 32 g; Fiber 6 g; T Fat 14 g;
Chol 0 mg; Sod 38 mg.*

*Phyllis F. Cannon
Virginia Beach, Virginia*

SPROUTS AND SPINACH SALAD

1/2 cup vinegar
1/4 cup sugar
1/2 teaspoon salt
3/4 cup olive oil
16 ounces fresh spinach, torn
1 16-ounce can bean
   sprouts, drained
3 green onions, sliced
1/2 8-ounce can sliced water
   chestnuts, drained
3 hard-boiled eggs, chopped
6 slices crisp-fried bacon,
   crumbled

Combine vinegar, sugar and salt in small bowl; mix until sugar and salt dissolve. Add olive oil; mix well. Chill until serving time. Combine spinach, bean sprouts, green onions, water chestnuts, eggs and bacon in salad bowl. Add dressing; toss to mix well. Yield: 6 servings.

*Approx Per Serving: Cal 386; Prot 8 g;
Carbo 17 g; Fiber 4 g; T Fat 33 g;
Chol 112 mg; Sod 383 mg.*

*Rita P. Kramer
Montebello High School
Montebello, California*

STRAWBERRY AND SPINACH SALAD

1/2 cup sugar
1 1/2 teaspoons onion flakes
1/4 teaspoon paprika
1/4 teaspoon Worcestershire
   sauce
1/2 cup oil
1/4 cup vinegar
2 tablespoons sesame seed
1 tablespoon poppy seed
2 pounds fresh spinach, torn
2 pints fresh strawberries,
   cut into halves

Combine sugar, onion flakes, paprika and Worcestershire sauce in blender container. Add oil and vinegar; process until smooth. Stir in sesame seed and poppy seed. Combine spinach and strawberries in salad bowl. Add dressing; toss to mix well. Yield: 12 servings.

*Approx Per Serving: Cal 154; Prot 3 g;
Carbo 15 g; Fiber 4 g; T Fat 10 g;
Chol 0 mg; Sod 62 mg.*

*Melissa Helbig
Republic High School
Republic, Missouri*

 A wooden salad bowl should never be washed. After each use, wipe it out thoroughly with a clean dry cloth, then with a piece of bread to absorb the oil. Before adding the salad ingredients, season the bowl by rubbing with warm oil then with a cut clove of garlic.

SUMMER SALAD

1/2 head lettuce, rinsed
1   8-ounce can mandarin
    oranges, drained
1/2 cup chopped pecans
1/4 cup Italian salad dressing

Tear lettuce into serving-sized pieces into salad bowl. Add mandarin oranges, pecans and salad dressing; toss lightly. Yield: 4 servings.

*Approx Per Serving: Cal 206; Prot 2 g;
Carbo 14 g; Fiber 2 g; T Fat 19 g;
Chol 0 mg; Sod 78 mg.*

*Carolyn Senac
Mandeville High School
Mandeville, Louisiana*

LAYERED GARDEN TOMATO SALAD

16 ounces mushrooms, sliced
1   8-ounce bottle of Italian
    salad dressing
1 medium head lettuce, torn
4 large tomatoes, chopped,
    drained
2 green onions, chopped
2 cups mayonnaise
2 cups shredded Cheddar
    cheese
1/4 cup bacon bits

Combine mushrooms with salad dressing in bowl. Marinate for 1 hour or longer; drain. Layer lettuce, tomatoes, mushrooms and green onions in large salad bowl. Spread mayonnaise over layers, sealing to edge of bowl. Top with cheese and bacon bits. Chill for several hours. Yield: 12 servings.

*Approx Per Serving: Cal 456; Prot 7 g;
Carbo 8 g; Fiber 2 g; T Fat 48 g;
Chol 42 mg; Sod 479 mg.
Nutritional information includes
entire amount of salad dressing marinade.*

*Doris S. Caldwell
Shawsville High School
Shawsville, Virginia*

 Fresh tarragon leaves are great served on tomato slices with a tart French dressing.

ZUCCHINI RELISH

4 cups thinly sliced zucchini
1/2 cup finely chopped green
   onions
1/2 cup soy sauce
1/4 cup vinegar
2 tablespoons oil
1/2 teaspoon sugar

Combine all ingredients in bowl; mix well. Chill, covered, for 1 hour to overnight. Yield: 4 servings.

*Approx Per Serving: Cal 104; Prot 4 g;
Carbo 9 g; Fiber 2 g; T Fat 7 g;
Chol 0 mg; Sod 2062 mg.*

*Susan Rogers
West High School
Torrance, California*

ANTIPASTO SALAD TOSS

1 7-ounce can artichoke
   hearts, drained, cut into
   halves
1 cup cherry tomato halves
1/2 cup sliced black olives
1/2 cup Italian salad dressing
6 cups torn salad greens
1 1/2 cups shredded
   mozzarella cheese
1 4-ounce package
   pepperoni slices
2 hard-boiled eggs, chopped

Combine artichokes, tomatoes and olives in bowl. Add salad dressing; mix well. Chill, covered, for several hours to overnight. Drain, reserving marinade. Combine with remaining ingredients in salad bowl. Drizzle with reserved marinade; toss to mix well. Yield: 8 servings.

*Approx Per Serving: Cal 261; Prot 10 g;
Carbo 7 g; Fiber 1 g; T Fat 24 g;
Chol 75 mg; Sod 586 mg.*

*Kathleen Ferro
Mountain Home Junior High School
Mountain Home, Arkansas*

ITALIAN VEGETABLES

2 cups broccoli flowerets
1 cup cauliflowerets
1 zucchini, diagonally sliced
1 cup cherry tomatoes, cut
   into quarters
1 cup sliced mushrooms
1/2 medium green bell
   pepper, sliced into rings
1/2 small onion, sliced into rings
1/2 cup sliced olives
1 8-ounce bottle of reduced-
   calorie Italian salad dressing

Combine broccoli, cauliflower, zucchini, tomatoes, mushrooms, green pepper, onion and olives in 2-quart bowl. Add salad dressing; toss lightly. Chill, covered, for 6 hours to several days, tossing occasionally. Yield: 6 servings.

*Approx Per Serving: Cal 80; Prot 2 g;
Carbo 8 g; Fiber 3 g; T Fat 6 g;
Chol 2 mg; Sod 454 mg.*

*Janiece Lee
Rockdale High School
Rockdale, Texas*

LITTLE VEGETABLE SALAD

1/2 cup oil
3/4 cup vinegar
1/2 cup sugar
1 teaspoon salt
1 teaspoon pepper
1 16-ounce can French-style
   green beans
1 15-ounce can tiny green
   peas
1 11-ounce can white corn
1 4-ounce jar chopped
   pimento
1 green bell pepper, chopped
1 cup chopped celery
1 cup chopped onion

Bring oil, vinegar, sugar, salt and pepper to a boil in saucepan, stirring to dissolve completely. Cool to room temperature. Drain beans, peas, corn and pimento. Combine with green pepper, celery and onion in large bowl. Add dressing; mix well. Yield: 10 servings.

*Approx Per Serving: Cal 213; Prot 4 g;
Carbo 27 g; Fiber 4 g; T Fat 12 g;
Chol 0 mg; Sod 504 mg.*

Susan S. Johnson
Vanguard High School
Ocala, Florida

MARINATED GARDEN SALAD

1 cup shredded cabbage
2 cups shredded lettuce
1 cup shredded carrots
1 cup chopped broccoli
1 cup chopped cauliflower
1 green bell pepper, chopped
1 cup sliced radishes
1/2 cup sliced green onions
1 cup mayonnaise
1/4 cup vinegar
2 tablespoons oil
1 envelope ranch salad
   dressing mix
2 teaspoons dillweed

Combine cabbage, lettuce, carrots, broccoli, cauliflower, green pepper, radishes and green onions in large salad bowl. Mix mayonnaise, vinegar, oil, dressing mix and dillweed in small bowl. Pour over salad; toss to coat well. Chill, tightly covered, overnight. Serve in individual salad bowls; garnish with tomato wedges or cherry tomatoes. Yield: 8 servings.

*Approx Per Serving: Cal 261; Prot 2 g;
Carbo 9 g; Fiber 2 g; T Fat 26 g;
Chol 16 mg; Sod 419 mg.*

Betty H. Knight
West Wilkes School
Millers Creek, North Carolina

 Keep chopped tomatoes for tossed salad in separate bowl. If there are salad greens left, they will stay nice and crisp.

MARINATED VEGETABLE SALAD

1 head lettuce, torn
Flowerets of 1 head cauliflower
Flowerets of 1 bunch broccoli
1 red onion, sliced
1 green bell pepper, sliced
  lengthwise
16 ounces fresh mushrooms,
  sliced
3 carrots, sliced
1 cucumber, sliced
1 pint cherry tomatoes
Garlic and Dill Dressing
  (page 118)

Combine lettuce, cauliflower, broccoli, onion, green pepper, mushrooms, carrots, cucumber and cherry tomatoes in large salad bowl; mix well. Add Garlic and Dill Dressing; toss lightly. Marinate in refrigerator for 1 hour. Yield: 15 servings.

Approx Per Serving: Cal 143; Prot 3 g; Carbo 10 g; Fiber 3 g; T Fat 11 g; Chol 0 mg; Sod 1020 mg.

Kathy Lynne Coakley
Bloom Carroll High School
Carroll, Ohio

SALAD MARINÉE

4 large carrots, sliced
3 green bell peppers, sliced
3 small onions, sliced
3 stalks celery, sliced
3 tomatoes, sliced
2 cucumbers, sliced
Basic French Dressing
  (page 117)

Layer carrots, green peppers, onions, celery, tomatoes and cucumbers in order listed in glass bowl. Pour Basic French Dressing over layers. Chill for several hours. Yield: 10 servings.

Approx Per Serving: Cal 250; Prot 2 g; Carbo 14 g; Fiber 3 g; T Fat 22 g; Chol 0 mg; Sod 708 mg.

Karen G. Smith
Northside High School
Warner Robins, Georgia

VEGETABLE SALAD

1 cup chopped broccoli
1 cup chopped cauliflower
1 cup thawed frozen green peas
1/4 cup chopped onion
1/4 cup chopped green bell
  pepper
1 cup shredded lettuce
1 cup mayonnaise
1 envelope Italian salad
  dressing mix

Combine first 6 ingredients in salad bowl. Mix mayonnaise and dressing mix in small bowl. Add to salad; toss lightly. Yield: 4 servings.

Approx Per Serving: Cal 444; Prot 4 g; Carbo 11 g; Fiber 4 g; T Fat 44 g; Chol 33 mg; Sod 604 mg.

Donna Frankenhauser
Santa Fe High School
Alachua, Florida

CENTRAL VALLEY SALAD

1 cup olive oil
¼ cup lemon juice
1½ teaspoons honey
1½ teaspoons Dijon mustard
1 teaspoon Worcestershire
   sauce
½ teaspoon salt
¼ teaspoon white pepper
1 large head romaine lettuce
4 ounces black grapes, cut
   into halves, seeded
Sections of 2 small oranges
1 small red onion, sliced
1 avocado, sliced

Combine olive oil, lemon juice, honey, mustard, Worcestershire sauce, salt and white pepper in covered jar; shake well to mix. Store, tightly covered, in refrigerator for up to 2 weeks. Toss lettuce with grapes, oranges, onion and avocado in salad bowl. Add dressing; toss lightly. Yield: 6 servings.

Approx Per Serving: Cal 428; Prot 2 g; Carbo 16 g; Fiber 6 g; T Fat 42 g; Chol 0 mg; Sod 210 mg.

Betty Ezell
Ramay Junior High School
Fayetteville, Arkansas

ORIENTAL VEGETABLE SALAD

1 cup sugar
1 cup tarragon vinegar
1   15-ounce can bamboo
   shoots
2   7-ounce cans sliced water
   chestnuts
1   16-ounce can bean sprouts
1   16-ounce can Chinese
   mixed vegetables
1   16-ounce can green peas
1   16-ounce can French-style
   green beans
1 cup thinly sliced onion
   rings
1 cup chopped celery

Bring sugar and vinegar to a boil in saucepan, stirring to dissolve sugar. Cool to room temperature. Drain bamboo shoots, water chestnuts, bean sprouts, mixed vegetables, peas and beans. Combine with onion rings and celery in salad bowl. Add dressing; toss lightly. Marinate in refrigerator for 24 hours. Yield: 12 servings.

Approx Per Serving: Cal 151; Prot 5 g; Carbo 35 g; Fiber 6 g; T Fat <1 g; Chol 0 mg; Sod 253 mg.

Ann McMullin
Smith-Cotton High School
Sedalia, Missouri

 Add a chopped pear (canned or fresh) and a bit of chopped onion to any mixture of salad greens and serve with vinaigrette dressing.

Salads Salads Salads Salads Salads
Salads Salads Salads Salads Salads
Salads Salads Salads Salads Salads
Salads Salads Salads Salads Salads

DRESSINGS

COOKED FRUIT DRESSING

1/4 cup butter
1/2 cup sugar
1 tablespoon lemon juice
3/4 cup pineapple juice
2 tablespoons orange juice
2 egg yolks, beaten
1 tablespoon cornstarch

Melt butter in top of double boiler. Add sugar, lemon juice, pineapple juice, orange juice and egg yolks; mix well. Stir in cornstarch. Cook until thickened, stirring constantly. Chill in refrigerator overnight. Yield: 30 tablespoons.

Approx Per Tablespoon: Cal 36; Prot <1 g; Carbo 5 g; Fiber <1 g; T Fat 2 g; Chol 18 mg; Sod 14 mg.

Shirley Davis
Rockwood High School
Rockwood, Tennessee

COOKED PINEAPPLE DRESSING

1/4 cup sugar
1/2 teaspoon salt
1 1/2 tablespoons flour
1 egg
2 tablespoons vinegar
3/4 cup pineapple juice

Combine all ingredients in saucepan; mix well. Cook over medium heat until thickened, stirring constantly. Chill until cold. Yield: 36 tablespoons.

Approx Per Tablespoon: Cal 12; Prot <1 g; Carbo 2 g; Fiber <1 g; T Fat <1 g; Chol 6 mg; Sod 32 mg.

Beverley C. Cole
Smyth County Vocational School
Marion, Virginia

COOKED WHIPPED CREAM DRESSING

1 egg
1 cup sugar
1/2 cup whipping cream
1/2 cup milk
1/8 teaspoon salt
1 1/2 teaspoons cornstarch
1 teaspoon vanilla extract

Combine egg, sugar, cream, milk, salt, cornstarch and vanilla in mixer bowl; beat until smooth. Pour into top of double boiler. Cook until slightly thickened, stirring constantly. Yield: 32 tablespoons.

Approx Per Tablespoon: Cal 43; Prot <1 g; Carbo 7 g; Fiber <1 g; T Fat 2 g; Chol 12 mg; Sod 14 mg.

Doris Stults
Collinwood High School
Collinwood, Tennessee

BASIC FRENCH DRESSING

1 clove of garlic
1/4 cup tomato sauce
1/3 cup red wine vinegar
1 tablespoon sugar
1 teaspoon each salt, basil
1 teaspoon Worcestershire
  sauce
1/4 teaspoon dry mustard
1/4 teaspoon ground pepper
1/8 teaspoon cayenne pepper
1 cup oil

Purée garlic in blender. Add next 9 ingredients. Process until blended. Add oil gradually, processing constantly at high speed until completely blended. Yield: 36 tablespoons.

Approx Per Tablespoon: Cal 56; Prot <1 g; Carbo 1 g; Fiber <1 g; T Fat 6 g; Chol 0 mg; Sod 69 mg.

Karen G. Smith
Northside High School
Warner Robins, Georgia

BLENDER TOMATO SOUP FRENCH DRESSING

1 cup sugar
1 teaspoon each salt,
  paprika, celery seed
1 cup tomato soup
1/2 cup vinegar
1 tablespoon each prepared
  mustard, Worcestershire
  sauce
1 cup oil

Combine first 8 ingredients in blender container. Process on medium speed until blended. Add oil gradually, processing constantly. Store in refrigerator. Yield: 64 tablespoons.

Approx Per Tablespoon: Cal 45; Prot <1 g; Carbo 4 g; Fiber <1 g; T Fat 3 g; Chol 0 mg; Sod 66 mg.

Mary Anne Fisher
Virginia Beach Junior High School
Virginia Beach, Virginia

SPICY FRENCH DRESSING

1/2 small onion
1 cup oil
2/3 cup catsup
1/2 cup cider vinegar
1/2 cup sugar
1 tablespoon lemon juice
1 teaspoon each salt, dry
  mustard and paprika
1/4 teaspoon garlic powder
1/8 teaspoon pepper

Cut onion into halves. Combine onion with remaining ingredients in blender container. Process at medium speed until well blended. May substitute 10 envelopes artificial sweetener for sugar to lower calorie count. Yield: 40 tablespoons.

Approx Per Tablespoon: Cal 64; Prot <1 g; Carbo 4 g; Fiber <1 g; T Fat 5 g; Chol 0 mg; Sod 100 mg.

Karen K. Burns
Santa Anna High School
Santa Anna, Texas

GARLIC AND DILL DRESSING

¾ cup oil
1 cup vinegar
1 teaspoon salt
1 teaspoon pepper
1 teaspoon dillseed
1 tablespoon sugar
1 tablespoon MSG
1 teaspoon minced garlic

Combine oil, vinegar, salt, pepper, dillseed, sugar, MSG and garlic in bowl; mix well. Yield: 30 tablespoons.

Approx Per Tablespoon: Cal 51; Prot 0 g; Carbo 1 g; Fiber 0 g; T Fat 5 g; Chol 0 mg; Sod 500 mg.

Kathy Lynne Coakley
Bloom Carroll High School
Carroll, Ohio

HOSFIELD'S HOUSE DRESSING

2 8-ounce bottles of Robusto salad dressing
1 8-ounce bottle of Wishbone Sweet and Spicey French salad dressing
4 ounces bleu cheese, crumbled

Drain oil from Robusto dressing; discard oil. Combine remaining Robusto dressing, Sweet and Spicey French dressing and bleu cheese in bowl; mix well. Store in dressing bottles in refrigerator. Yield: 50 tablespoons.

Approx Per Tablespoon: Cal 32; Prot 1 g; Carbo <1 g; Fiber <1 g; T Fat 3 g; Chol 2 mg; Sod 85 mg.

Chris Hornbed
S. M. South School
Overland Park, Kansas

KOREAN SALAD DRESSING

1 cup oil
¾ cup sugar
⅓ cup catsup
1 teaspoon Worcestershire sauce
1 medium onion, sliced
½ teaspoon salt
¼ cup dark vinegar

Combine oil, sugar, catsup, Worcestershire sauce, onion, salt and vinegar in blender container. Process at high speed until well blended. Yield: 50 tablespoons.

Approx Per Tablespoon: Cal 53; Prot <1 g; Carbo 4 g; Fiber <1 g; T Fat 4 g; Chol 0 mg; Sod 41 mg.

Pamela Cormany
Adena High School
Frankfort, Ohio

NANCY'S FAVORITE SALAD DRESSING

2 eggs, beaten
2 tablespoons sugar
1/3 cup water
1/3 cup vinegar
1/2 teaspoon salt

Combine all ingredients in heavy saucepan; mix well. Bring to a boil, stirring constantly. Cook for 2 to 3 minutes or until thickened, stirring constantly. Chill until serving time. Yield: 15 tablespoons.

Approx Per Tablespoon: Cal 18; Prot 1 g; Carbo 2 g; Fiber 0 g; T Fat 1 g; Chol 28 mg; Sod 80 mg.

Nancy H. Elvetici
Wythe County Vocational School
Wytheville, Virginia

COLESLAW DRESSING

2 cups mayonnaise-type
  salad dressing
1/2 cup vinegar
1/2 cup sugar
1 teaspoon salt
2 teaspoons celery salt

Combine all ingredients in bowl; mix well. Add enough dressing to shredded cabbage to moisten. Store in airtight container in refrigerator. Yield: 48 tablespoons.

Approx Per Tablespoon: Cal 47; Prot <1 g; Carbo 5 g; Fiber 0 g; T Fat 3 g; Chol 3 mg; Sod 203 mg.

Annette Smith
Houston High School
Houston, Missouri

SLAW DRESSING

1/4 cup mayonnaise
2 tablespoons sugar
1 tablespoon vinegar
Salt and pepper to taste

Combine mayonnaise, sugar, vinegar, salt and pepper in jar. Cover with lid. Shake until well blended. Chill until serving time. Yield: 7 tablespoons.

Approx Per Tablespoon: Cal 70; Prot <1 g; Carbo 4 g; Fiber 0 g; T Fat 6 g; Chol 5 mg; Sod 45 mg.

Dorothy Hawk
Sullivan Central High School
Blountville, Tennessee

SWEET SESAME DRESSING

3/4 teaspoon Italian
  seasoning mix
1 1/2 teaspoons paprika
1 tablespoon sesame seed
1 1/2 teaspoons salt
1/4 teaspoon pepper
2 cups vinegar
2 cups sugar
1/2 cup oil

Combine Italian seasoning mix, paprika, sesame seed, salt, pepper, vinegar and sugar in bowl; mix well. Add oil; mix well. Serve on pasta salad. Yield: 70 tablespoons.

Approx Per Tablespoon: Cal 37; Prot <1 g; Carbo 6 g; Fiber <1 g; T Fat 2 g; Chol 0 mg; Sod 49 mg.

Jean Ann Sadler
Southside High School
Fort Smith, Arkansas

SWEET AND SOUR DRESSING

1 11-ounce can mandarin
  oranges, drained
1/4 cup oil
2 tablespoons sugar
1 tablespoon minced parsley
1/2 teaspoon salt
1/8 teaspoon hot pepper sauce
1/8 teaspoon pepper

Combine mandarin oranges, oil, sugar, parsley, salt, hot pepper sauce and pepper in jar with cover. Shake, covered, until well mixed. Store in refrigerator. Yield: 16 tablespoons.

Approx Per Tablespoon: Cal 48; Prot <1 g; Carbo 5 g; Fiber <1 g; T Fat 3 g; Chol 0 mg; Sod 68 mg.

Terri Holder
C. E. King High School
Houston, Texas

THOUSAND ISLAND DRESSING

1 1/2 cups mayonnaise
1/2 cup sweet pickle relish
1 1/4 cups catsup

Combine mayonnaise, pickle relish and catsup in bowl; mix well. May store, covered, in refrigerator for several weeks. Yield: 50 tablespoons.

Approx Per Tablespoon: Cal 58; Prot <1 g; Carbo 3 g; Fiber <1 g; T Fat 5 g; Chol 4 mg; Sod 126 mg.

Judy Henke
Nickerson High School
Nickerson, Kansas

CHERYL'S VEGETABLE DRESSING

1 cup mayonnaise
1/2 cup sour cream
1/4 teaspoon salt
1/4 teaspoon paprika
1/2 teaspoon garlic powder
1/2 teaspoon lemon juice
1/2 teaspoon Worcestershire
   sauce
1 teaspoon parsley flakes
1 tablespoon Salad Supreme
   seasoning

Combine all ingredients in bowl; mix well.
Chill, covered, for several hours before serving.
May also be used as a dip for vegetables.
Yield: 24 tablespoons.

*Approx Per Tablespoon: Cal 76; Prot <1 g;
Carbo <1 g; Fiber <1 g; T Fat 8 g;
Chol 8 mg; Sod 78 mg.*

*Mary Myer
Basehor-Linwood High School
Basehor, Kansas*

VEGETABLE SALAD DRESSING

2 cups mayonnaise
1 envelope ranch party dip
   mix
1 cup sour cream

Combine mayonnaise, dip mix and sour cream
in bowl; mix well. Serve with vegetable salad.
Yield: 40 tablespoons.

*Approx Per Tablespoon: Cal 93; Prot <1 g;
Carbo 1 g; Fiber 0 g; T Fat 10 g;
Chol 9 mg; Sod 114 mg.*

*Nancy Thornsberry
Unioto High School
Chillicothe, Ohio*

BLEU CHEESE VINAIGRETTE

6 tablespoons oil
3 tablespoons white wine
   vinegar
3 tablespoons crumbled bleu
   cheese
1/4 teaspoon salt
1/4 teaspoon dry mustard
1/8 teaspoon pepper

Combine oil, vinegar, bleu cheese, salt, mustard
and pepper in jar with cover. Shake, covered,
until well blended. Chill until serving time.
Yield: 12 tablespoons.

*Approx Per Tablespoon: Cal 65; Prot <1 g;
Carbo <1 g; Fiber 0 g; T Fat 7 g;
Chol 1 mg; Sod 61 mg.*

*M. Joanne Hughes
Shawnee Mission North High School
Shawnee Mission, Kansas*

GARLIC VINAIGRETTE

2 tablespoons vinegar
1/4 cup oil
2 or 3 drops of Worcestershire
  sauce
1/8 teaspoon salt
1/8 teaspoon pepper
1/8 teaspoon garlic powder

Combine vinegar, oil, Worcestershire sauce, salt, pepper and garlic powder in jar with cover. Shake, covered, until well blended. Chill until serving time. Yield: 6 tablespoons.

Approx Per Tablespoon: Cal 81; Prot <1 g; Carbo <1 g; Fiber 0 g; T Fat 9 g; Chol 0 mg; Sod 50 mg.

Virginia Dare Garber
Grundy Senior High School
Grundy, Virginia

ORANGE VINAIGRETTE

1/2 cup oil
1/4 cup cider vinegar
1 teaspoon sugar
1 teaspoon grated orange rind
1/4 cup orange juice
1 clove of garlic, minced
1 tablespoon minced parsley
1/2 teaspoon curry powder
1/2 teaspoon pepper
1/2 teaspoon ginger
1/2 teaspoon paprika

Combine oil, vinegar, sugar, orange rind, orange juice, garlic, parsley, curry powder, pepper, ginger and paprika in bowl; mix well. Store, covered, in refrigerator. Yield: 16 tablespoons.

Approx Per Tablespoon: Cal 64; Prot <1 g; Carbo 1 g; Fiber <1 g; T Fat 7 g; Chol 0 mg; Sod <1 mg.

Linda Wahlberg
Franklin County High School
Rocky Mount, Virginia

RICE VINEGAR DRESSING

1/4 cup rice vinegar
1/2 teaspoon brown sugar
1/8 teaspoon ginger
3 tablespoons water
1 tablespoon oil
1 1/2 teaspoons frozen orange
  juice concentrate, thawed
1/2 teaspoon dark sesame oil
1/2 teaspoon low-sodium soy
  sauce

Combine rice vinegar, brown sugar, ginger, water, oil, orange juice concentrate, sesame oil and soy sauce in bowl; mix well.
Yield: 8 tablespoons.

Approx Per Tablespoon: Cal 22; Prot <1 g; Carbo 1 g; Fiber <1 g; T Fat 2 g; Chol 0 mg; Sod 16 mg.

Lenore Hamilton
Naperville Central High School
Naperville, Illinois

Index

AMBROSIA
Bubbly Ambrosia, 26
Low-Calorie Ambrosia, 26

APRICOT
Apricot Salad, 27
Pineapple and Apricot Salad, 27
Sweet and Creamy Apricot Mold, 28

ASPARAGUS
Asparagus and Pea Salad, 80
Asparagus Toss, 80

BANANA
Banana and Date Salad, 28
Frozen Banana Salad, 29

BEAN
Green Bean and Corn Salad, 81
Green Bean Salad, 80
Italian Chick-Pea Salad, 90
Pea and Green Bean Salad, 99
Scandinavian Bean Salad, 81

BEEF
Sirloin Steak Salad, 10
Super Simple Roast Beef Salad, 10
Tabouli Salad, 17

BLUEBERRY
Blueberry Gelatin Salad, 29
Cherry and Blueberry Salad, 30
Raspberry and Blueberry Salad, 30

BROCCOLI
Broccoli and Cauliflower Salad, 82
Broccoli and Cheddar Salad, 82
Broccoli and Mushroom Salad, 83
Broccoli and Pecan Salad, 82
Broccoli and Swiss Cheese Salad, 83
Broccoli Salad, 84
Cauliflower and Broccoli Salad, 87
Christmas Vegetable Salad, 88

CABBAGE
Chinese Slaw, 85
Crunchy Hawaiian Salad, 84
Marinated Cabbage Slaw, 85
Really Different Slaw, 86

CARROT
Copper Penny Salad, 86
Orange and Carrot Salad, 87
Sunshine Salad, 87

CAULIFLOWER
Broccoli and Cauliflower Salad, 82
Cauliflower and Broccoli Salad, 87
Cauliflower and Cheddar Salad, 89
Cauliflower Confetti Salad, 88
Cauliflower Salad, 89
Christmas Vegetable Salad, 88
Parmesan Cauliflower Salad, 89

CHERRY
Cherry and Blueberry Salad, 30
Cherry Fruit Salad, 32
Cherry Salad, 31
Cherry Snowball Ring Mold, 32
Pretty Pink Salad, 33

CHICKEN
Chicken Liver Salad, 13
Chicken Noodle-Tuna Salad, 23
Chicken Salad, 11
Chicken Salad with Olives, 12
Cold Curried Chicken Salad, 11
Curried Chicken Salad, 12
Hot Chicken Salad, 13
Main Dish Pasta Salad, 68
Oriental Fried Chicken Salad, 14
Oriental Sesame Chicken Salad, 14
Ramen Chicken and Cabbage Salad, 15
Shrimp Salad, 21
Thai Mixed Salad, 15

CONGEALED
Apricot Salad, 27
Berry Salad, 47
Blueberry Gelatin Salad, 29
Buttermilk Salad, 31
Champagne Salad, 31
Cherry and Blueberry Salad, 30
Cherry Snowball Ring Mold, 32
Christmas Rainbow Salad, 39
Cran-Raspberry Ring, 34
Fresh Cranberry Salad, 34
Fresh Strawberry-Pretzel Salad, 53
Fruit Salad, 46

Gooseberry Salad, 37
Heavenly Orange Fluff, 40
Light Waldorf Gelatin Salad, 56
Lime Gelatin Salad, 38
Lime Walnut Salad, 39
Nutty Cranberry and Fruit
    Gelatin, 35
Orange Fruit Salad, 41
Orange Pretzel Salad, 42
Orange Sherbet Congealed Salad, 43
Peach Gelatin Salad, 43
Pear Salad, 44
Pineapple and Apricot Salad, 27
Pretzel Salad, 54
Raspberries and Cream Salad, 47
Raspberry and Blueberry Salad, 30
Raspberry-Pretzel Salad, 48
Red Raspberry Salad, 48
Red Salad, 49
Rhubarb Salad, 49
Sawdust Salad, 45
Seven-Up Gelatin Salad, 50
Seven-Up Salad, 50
Strawberry Delight, 55
Strawberry Fluff, 52
Strawberry Salad, 55
Strawberry-Pretzel Congealed
    Salad, 54
Strawberry-Pretzel Salad, 53
Sweet and Creamy Apricot Mold, 28
Tasty Cranberry Salad, 36

CORN
Cold Corn Salad, 91
Corn Salad, 91
Green Bean and Corn Salad, 81

CORN BREAD
Cheesy Corn Bread Salad, 90
Mexican Corn Bread Salad, 91

CRANBERRY
Cran-Raspberry Ring, 34
Cranberry Salad, 36
Fresh Cranberry Salad, 34
Frozen Cranberry Salad, 35
Merry Cranberry Freeze, 33
Nutty Cranberry and Fruit Gelatin, 35
Tasty Cranberry Salad, 36

CUCUMBER
Company Cucumber Salad, 92
Cucumber Salad, 92
Turkish Cucumber Salad, 93

FROZEN
Creamy Frozen Fruit Salad, 60
Frozen Banana Salad, 29
Frozen Cranberry Salad, 35
Frozen Fruit Loaf, 60
Frozen Fruit Salad, 59
Frozen Lime Mint Salad, 38
Frozen Party Salad, 61
Kay's Frozen Fruit Salad, 61
Merry Cranberry Freeze, 33
Snowball Salad, 51

FRUIT, MIXED
Bubbly Ambrosia, 26
Cherry Fruit Salad, 32
Colorful Fruit Salad, 58
Creamy Fruit Salad, 58
Five-Cup Salad, 37
Florida Winter Salad, 58
Fresh Fruit Salad with Orange
    Cream, 59
Fruit Compote, 62
Fruit Salad, 62
Fruit Slush, 63
Hawaiian Fruit Cocktail, 64
Hawaiian Salad, 51
Low-Calorie Ambrosia, 26
Make-Ahead Fruit Salad, 64
Mama's Fruit Salad, 65
Melon Salad, 40
Mexican Fruit Salad, 56
Mother-in-Law's Fruit Salad, 65
My Sour Cream Fruit Salad, 65
Our Family Fruit Salad, 66
Quick Fruit Yum, 66
Six-Cup Salad, 51
Tasty Fruit Salad, 63
Watergate Salad, 57
White Salad, 57
Yummy Fruit Salad, 66

GROUND BEEF
Easy Taco Salad, 16
Personal Taco Salad, 16
Ranch Salad, 17

HAM
Chef's Pasta Salad, 73
Main Dish Ham Salad, 18
Pasta Salad with Ham, 75
Regina's Quick Pasta Salad, 73

LETTUCE, LAYERED
Layered Salad, 94

Layered Salad with Avocado, 94
Overnight Salad, 96
Twenty-Four Hour Vegetable Salad, 97

LETTUCE, TOSSED
Greens with Orange Vinaigrette, 94
Mandarin Orange Tossed Salad, 95
Mock Caesar Salad, 93
Orange and Green Delight, 96
Romaine Salad with Mandarin
    Oranges, 95
Summer Salad, 110

LIME
Best Green Salad, 44
Frozen Lime Mint Salad, 38
Lime Gelatin Salad, 38
Lime Walnut Salad, 39

MUSHROOM
Broccoli and Mushroom Salad, 83
Fresh Mushroom Salad, 97
Mushroom and Orange Salad, 98

ORANGE
Heavenly Orange Fluff, 40
Mandarin Orange Tossed Salad, 95
Mushroom and Orange Salad, 98
Orange and Carrot Salad, 87
Orange and Green Delight, 96
Orange Fluff, 41
Orange Fruit Salad, 41
Orange Pretzel Salad, 42
Orange Refrigerator Salad, 42
Orange Sherbet Congealed Salad, 43
Romaine Salad with Mandarin
    Oranges, 95
Summer Salad, 110

PASTA
Cheddar Macaroni Salad, 71
Chef's Pasta Salad, 73
English Pea and Pasta Salad, 68
Frog Eye Salad, 69
Italian Pasta and Salmon Salad, 70
Italian Sausage and Pasta Salad, 69
Italian Spaghetti Salad, 77
Italian Vegetable Toss, 70
Lemon Spaghetti Salad, 78
Macaroni Salad, 72
Main Dish Pasta Salad, 68
Mexican Pasta Salad, 74
Oriental Tortelini Salad, 78
Pasta and Bean Salad, 74

Pasta and Vegetable Medley, 76
Pasta Salad, 68
Pasta Salad with Ham, 75
Pasta Salad with Shrimp, 75
Regina's Quick Pasta Salad, 73
Rotini Salad, 72
Spaghetti Salad, 77
Stir-Fry Vegetable-Style Linquine, 71
Tuna-Macaroni Salad, 72
Vegetable and Pasta Salad, 76

PEA
English Pea and Pasta Salad, 68
Green Pea Salad, 99
Lone Star Caviar, 98
Pea and Green Bean Salad, 99
Pea-Nut Salad, 99

PINEAPPLE
Fruit Salad, 46
Pineapple Salad, 46
Pineapple-Cheese Salad, 45
Sawdust Salad, 45

POTATO
Cottage Cheese Potato Salad, 100
German Potato Salad, 100
Layered Potato Salad, 101
Lean Potato Salad, 101
Sour Cream Potato Salad, 102

RASPBERRY
Berry Salad, 47
Raspberries and Cream Salad, 47
Raspberry and Blueberry Salad, 30
Raspberry-Pretzel Salad, 48
Red Raspberry Salad, 48
Red Salad, 49

RICE
Favorite Rice Salad, 102
Lemony Rice Salad, 103
Rice-A-Roni, 103
Tuna Rice Mix-Up, 23

SALAD DRESSINGS
Cheryl's Vegetable Dressing, 121
Coleslaw Dressing, 119
Garlic and Dill Dressing, 118
Hosfield's House Dressing, 118
Korean Salad Dressing, 118
Nancy's Favorite Salad Dressing, 119
Slaw Dressing, 119
Sweet and Sour Dressing, 120

Sweet Sesame Dressing, 120
Thousand Island Dressing, 120
Varied Salad Dressing, 81
Vegetable Salad Dressing, 121

SALAD DRESSINGS, COOKED
Cooked Fruit Dressing, 116
Cooked Pineapple Dressing, 116
Cooked Whipped Cream Dressing, 116

SALAD DRESSINGS, FRENCH
Basic French Dressing, 117
Blender Tomato Soup French
    Dressing, 117
Spicy French Dressing, 117

SALAD DRESSINGS, VINAIGRETTE
Bleu Cheese Vinaigrette, 121
Garlic Vinaigrette, 122
Orange Vinaigrette, 122
Rice Vinegar Dressing, 122

SAUERKRAUT
Kraut Salad, 104
Sweet Sauerkraut Salad, 104

SAUSAGE
Italian Sausage and Pasta Salad, 69
Pasta and Bean Salad, 74
Sausage Skillet Salad, 18

SEAFOOD. *See also* Shrimp; Tuna
Italian Pasta and Salmon Salad, 70
Spanish Shrimp and Scallop Salad, 19
Stuffed Tomatoes with Crab Meat
    Dressing, 19

SHRIMP
Crunchy Shrimp Salad, 20
Pasta Salad with Shrimp, 75
Shrimp and Orange Salad, 20
Shrimp and Rice Salad, 20
Shrimp Mold, 21
Shrimp Salad, 21
Shrimp Sea Breeze, 22
Spanish Shrimp and Scallop Salad, 19

SLAW
Chinese Slaw, 85
Marinated Cabbage Slaw, 85
Really Different Slaw, 86

SPINACH
Fresh Spinach Salad, 105

Fruited Spinach Salad, 108
Greens with Orange Vinaigrette, 94
Korean Salad, 105
Layered Salad, 94
Oriental Spinach Salad with Tuna, 22
Spinach and Apple Salad, 107
Spinach and Pecan Salad, 106
Spinach Salad, 106
Spinach Salad with Spicy Dressing, 107
Spring Spinach Salad, 108
Sprouts and Spinach Salad, 109
Strawberry and Spinach Salad, 109
Viva Tuna Spinach Salad, 24

STRAWBERRY
Fresh Strawberry-Pretzel Salad, 53
Light Cottage Cheese Salad, 52
Pretzel Salad, 54
Strawberry and Spinach Salad, 109
Strawberry Delight, 55
Strawberry Fluff, 52
Strawberry Salad, 55
Strawberry-Pretzel Congealed Salad, 54
Strawberry-Pretzel Salad, 53

TACO
Easy Taco Salad, 16
Personal Taco Salad, 16
Ranch Salad, 17
Turkey Taco Salad, 24

TUNA
Chicken Noodle-Tuna Salad, 23
Oriental Spinach Salad with Tuna, 22
Tuna Rice Mix-Up, 23
Tuna-Macaroni Salad, 72
Viva Tuna Spinach Salad, 24

VEGETABLE. *See also* Individual Kinds
Antipasto Salad Toss, 111
Central Valley Salad, 114
Italian Vegetables, 111
Italian Vegetable Toss, 70
Layered Garden Tomato Salad, 110
Little Vegetable Salad, 112
Marinated Garden Salad, 112
Marinated Vegetable Salad, 113
Oriental Vegetable Salad, 114
Pasta and Vegetable Medley, 76
Salad Marinée, 113
Stir-Fry Vegetable-Style Linguine, 71
Vegetable and Pasta Salad, 76
Vegetable Salad, 113
Zucchini Relish, 111

LIONS IN THE KITCHEN

This Cookbook is a perfect gift for Holidays, Weddings, Anniversaries and Birthdays.

You may order as many of our *Lions in the Kitchen* Cookbooks as you wish for the price of $8.00 each, plus $2.00 postage and handling per book ordered and mailed within the U.S.A. Mail to:

**Huntsville Lions Club
P.O. Box 162
Huntsville, Alabama 35804**

Make checks payable to the order of:
Huntsville Lions Club

Please indicate:

Total books ordered _____ Amount enclosed _____

Ship to:

NAME_____

ADDRESS _____

CITY_____ STATE _____ZIP_____